The Swish:
An In-Depth Look at this Powerful NLP Pattern

Shawn Carson

Jess Marion

Forward by John Overdurf

© 2013 by Shawn Carson, Jess Marion

The Swish: An In Depth Look at this Powerful NLP Pattern

NLP Mastery Series

Changing Minds Publishing. All rights reserved.

Cover design Richie Williams
Interior book design by Nancy Rawlinson

No part of this book may be reproduced in any manner whatsoever without written permission except in the case of brief quotations embedded in critical articles and reviews. For further information, please contact **Changing Mind Publishing** at 545 8th Ave, Suite 930, New York, NY 10001.

Table of Contents

TABLE OF CONTENTS

Introduction 11
The History of the Swish Pattern 18
A Brief Example of the Swish Pattern 23
How the Swish Pattern Works....................................31
The Swish Pattern in Detail..36
Finding the Problem Context and the Trigger 40
Creating the New Self-Image.....................................49
Using Archetypes 58
Designing the Swish Pattern using Submodalities...63
Delivering the Swish Pattern using
Gestures and Voice 69
Combining the Swish Pattern with the
New Behavior Generator 73
The Swish Pattern as a Recovery Strategy 84
The Hypnotic Swish Pattern 90
The Conversational Swish Pattern 103
The Social Swish Pattern..112
The Physical Swish Pattern 120
The Self-Coaching Swish Pattern
for Personal Success..126
The Swish Pattern for Business 137

The Swish Pattern for Dealing with
Difficult People..143

The Swish Pattern for Smoking and Other Habits ..150

Stepping into the Future..158

About the Authors..161

Acknowledgments...162

Glossary..163

Preface

I don't remember exactly where we were when Jess Marion and I began to discuss the genesis for this book on the Swish Pattern, the first in a series of books on NLP Mastery. It is very likely that the conversation took place somewhere pleasant and outdoors—perhaps the Mirror Pond in New York's Central Park, or the 70th Street Pier on the West Side of Manhattan, where we go with my wife, Sarah, and perhaps a few friends, to watch the sun setting over the skyline of Jersey City.

Over a glass or two of cold beer, we were discussing how many ways NLP patterns such as the Swish can be done with clients, how unfortunate it is that we really only have time to teach one way of doing each pattern when we are running an NLP Practitioner course, and how it is surprising that, while there are many books describing NLP patterns, nobody (at least as far as we know) has ever thought to write a book about all the nuances of one specific NLP pattern. Of course, we realized that that "nobody" included us, so rather than complain about it, we would just have to write it ourselves!

Jess and I agreed that we would each prepare a first draft of a manuscript on a separate pattern and then exchange them for review, thereby having two books co-written. Jess was fascinated by the Visual Squash, but for me there was only one choice: the Swish.

I learned and practiced the steps of the Swish many years ago during my NLP Practitioner training in New York City. But I didn't learn the true power of the Swish until I saw it demonstrated on a fellow student by an incredible NLP Master Trainer named John Overdurf. The beginning was simple: John asked for a volunteer with a small problem, such as procrastination about studying—the type of small issue we all face everyday. Then, suddenly, seemingly far above that, he asked a single question: "How do you want to be different, and how will you be as a person when you are?" Then John took each phrase the student offered and sweetened it into a possibility, into an image of such delight! This was a kind of NLP I had never seen! Even though I was just an observer, I was filled with a longing to step into that possible future self, as if I were seeing the universe showing me my own potential.

The Swish Pattern allows a client to work through the most minor and mundane issues and emerge on the far side transformed. Like a pearl forming inside an oyster, the problem becomes the grit that is transformed, through the alchemy of the Swish Pattern, into the new you. After all, if you are going to change one thing, why not change everything?

—Shawn Carson
New York City, 2013

Foreword

It is my great pleasure to introduce this valuable work by Shawn Carson and Jess Marion. I'm going to tell you right out of the gate: you're going to be glad you read this book. It is worth its weight in CHANGE.

I've been fortunate to know Shawn for many years now. His NYC-Brit wit is so dry I was never sure about whether I should take him seriously or not—so I decided to! Probably the highest compliment I can give to someone in our field is saying, "You are a true student of the game." That's Shawn: competent, passionate, and dedicated, with the humility that comes from having a glimpse of a bigger picture and from not taking himself too seriously.

I met Jess, a student of Shawn and his wife Sarah's, at a hypnosis training I was doing in New York City last fall. Her warm smile greeted me on the first day, and by the end of the training I realized I'd found another "student of the game"—a testament to her, her teachers, and the idea that "you never know how far a change will go."

This is a book for true students of the game, written by two true students of the game. It is about one of the most flexible and versatile change patterns in the classic NLP repertoire: The Swish. Oh, and did I mention? You never know how far a change will go.

Shawn and Jess take the Swish by storm. No stone is left unturned. This is one thorough treatment! It's concise, yet deep. Demos, practical tips for using the pattern in a variety of ways, in a variety of settings – it's all here.

Why Read this Book?

Hmm, let's see. Imagine asking a client—or yourself:

How cool would it be to take any situation that gives you some trouble and use it to catapult yourself toward a new way of being?

Would you like to significantly increase the pleasure you feel in life by exercising and strengthening the pleasure circuitry in your brain? (More about that in a bit.)

Do you have any long-term projects? Do you want to stay motivated and moving toward a successful completion?

Would you like to transform some unproductive habits into new, productive ones?

Interested? Might as well be, right? After all, you never know how far...

The process of the Swish is a simple one, but there are lots of nuances and variations you can learn to really maximize its effectiveness—but I'll leave that to Shawn and Jess! In its most basic form, the Swish is about linking two pictures together in your mind's eye. The first is the trigger for the "limitation" you want to change and the second is a new self-image of how you want to be. Through the process, the trigger for the problem becomes the trigger for the new self-image. Your brain goes gets re-routed toward a NEW YOU. The Swish wires in an entirely new self-image. *You can build new capabilities, new personal qualities, new beliefs, new values, and a new identity all in one fell swoop – or Swish!*

Make a sWISH Before You Read this Book

I don't know about you, but for me, when I begin to read a book, there is a certain sense of anticipation: you look at the cover and maybe page through it a bit to whet your appetite for something really tasty. What you don't know for sure is how much you'll learn, or how different you will be by the time you finish the book—but obviously there's something that you want to achieve, or you wouldn't be reading this right now.

Most of us were never taught one simple thing that we can do in order to read faster and with greater comprehension and deeper impact. Want to know what that thing is?

It's this: Ask yourself questions before you read the book.

What new thing would you like to learn? What are you curious about, regarding the Swish? How would you be different, having thoroughly read this book and gotten what you wanted from it? How would you be as a person, having integrated all this? Get the picture of yourself being that way.

Then check out the table of contents and quickly page through the book. Just graze. Resist diving right into something you think is interesting. You're creating anticipation and purpose. Doing this primes your brain to not just absorb information, but suck it in like a Dyson vacuum cleaner. At a deep level, as you turn the pages, you're activating that picture you made. (By the way, that is not a suggestion—more of a statement of how your brain works.)

Each time you open the book, having that sense of anticipation lights up a region in your brain commonly known as the dopamine pleasure circuit. This is the exact same circuitry that the Swish engages so effectively. This circuit thrives on novelty and gets exercised whenever you are feeling anticipation, excitement, or the rush of wanting to "go for it."

The Swish as a Dopamine Driver

Dopamine is the neurotransmitter that gives you the "go for it" feeling. It's the rush you get when you really feel alive. Ever been attracted to someone and felt like you were just being drawn toward that person? The closer you got, the more intense the feeling became, right? How about when you think about an upcoming vacation or trip—getting to go to some place you've never experienced before, and you're counting the days? That's all dopamine. Lit-up dopamine-using neurons are what create drive and motivation.

Deep in the center of your brain lies the ventral tegmental area (VTA). The VTA is filled with dopamine-using neurons that extend all the way to the nucleus accumbens (your pleasure center), the amygdala (your emotional amplifier), the hippocampus (your memory depot—so you can record your pleasure) and the prefrontal lobe (so you can connect all this to your self-image and what's important to you).

When you do the Slingshot Swish, one variation that Shawn and Jess teach you, you will be exercising that circuit. And there's more! Neuroscience has documented that the neurons in our brains are more like our muscles than we ever knew: they can be trained to grow in size. This is known as neuroplasticity. Our brain is an organ and our mind is our attention. Our brains are constantly re-wiring themselves through our life experience, but we can also use our minds to change our brains.

The Swish Pattern is one of the easiest ways to harness this neuroplasticity. You are re-wiring your brain in a very simple and direct way with the Swish. Furthermore, each time you repeat the process, you are actually causing the activated neurons to grow in size, fire more easily and more quickly, and connect to more of their neighbors. You are creating a new circuit and training your dopaminepleasure circuit at the same time.

Don't you think you could make room for more pleasure and drive in your life? Want to know all the nuances and details about how you can use the Swish to help yourself and others? Let Shawn and Jess show you, and remember what happens when you're willing to turn the page. *You never know...*

sWishing YOU a life of pleasure, possibility, peace by peace,

—John Overdurf
Arizona, 2013

Introduction

This book examines, in depth, one of the fundamental patterns of Neuro-Linguistic Programming, or NLP: the Swish Pattern. As such, this book will benefit all coaches, hypnotists, and therapists who use NLP in their practices. It's also a useful guide for people with a passing knowledge of NLP techniques who wish to develop their expertise further.

To understand why it is important to examine any NLP pattern in detail in this way, consider the following benefits:

1) You will gain a thorough and in-depth understanding of the pattern itself. Although the Swish is described elsewhere, we are not aware of any book that describes the pattern in enough detail to do it justice. You may wish to know how to use the Swish elegantly for a number of different client issues or contexts. Or you may simply want a very thorough and deep understanding of the mechanics of the Swish so that you can adapt it easily to any situation. Whatever your reason, this book will provide the level of information you really need.

2) You will begin to see the underlying functioning of the mind. You will also discover how the NLP techniques underlying the Swish Pattern work within the mind to create change. You will understand how submodalities work and how to use them to both release negative emotions and build up positive ones in their place. You will also understand how an emotion can be destructive in one context but a strong resource in another. But perhaps the greatest understanding that comes from studying the

Swish is how self-identity relates to personal change. At its core, the Swish is designed to install a new self-identity in the client. Building this new self-identity on a deep, unconscious level provides a new framework within which generative changes develop. As NLP Master Trainer John Overdurf says, you never know how far a change may go! This is particularly true of the Swish.

3) You will begin to extend your own coaching flexibility. You might use the Swish in any number of contexts: NLP coaching, a hypnosis session, business coaching, or simply working with a friend. Perhaps you are curious about how to use the Swish Pattern in a conversational way, such as in a business relationship where the Classical Swish may not be appropriate. Or, if you are a classically trained hypnotist, you may be curious about how to incorporate the Swish Pattern into deep trance work. If you are interested in personal development, you may wish to know how to use the Swish Pattern for yourself. This book provides detailed instructions for using the Swish in any context. So, now that you are ready to begin, let's start by putting the Swish Pattern into context within the evolution of NLP.

What is NLP?

Neuro-Linguistic Programming (NLP) is based upon the study of the brain and body, and of how the wiring of each individual's brain and nervous system (neuro) and use of language (linguistic) shapes that individual's personal reality on a systematic basis (programming). By first understanding and then systematically changing the way that you think about the world, you can change the wiring of your brain. This process is called self-directed neuroplasticity. NLP is a discipline that provides the specific tools you need to rewire your brain and achieve your dreams and goals.

NLP provides a set of techniques based on modeling states of excellence. It is used by coaches, therapists, and hypnotists to help others be the best that they can be. It is also used by business people, athletes and artists. In fact, the techniques of NLP are useful to anyone who recognizes that there are limitations they want to overcome in order to attain excellence in their lives.

NLP was developed in the 1970s by Richard Bandler and John Grinder. Bandler and Grinder noticed that some therapists excelled in helping their clients to change. They concluded that if they could identify what made these therapists great, they could build a "model" of techniques and communication that others could adopt, and then change could happen more easily for everyone. As a result, Bandler and Grinder "modeled" some of the best therapists practicing at the time, people such as Fritz Perls, Virginia Satir and Milton Erickson.

It was from these models that techniques like the Swish Pattern evolved. Patterns such as the Swish are among the most well known aspects of NLP. They are designed to use the natural software of the human brain to produce optimal results and achieve change. But as much as the details of the techniques are important, the spirit in which they are undertaken matters too.

A definition of NLP widely attributed to Richard Bandler is "an attitude of wanton experimentation which leaves behind a trail of techniques." If you ever get the chance to watch Richard Bandler in action, you'll understand what he means by that! Bandler is a whirlwind of creative energy. He becomes intensely curious about the people in front of him. He wants to know how they do what they do, and how they construct their map of reality. His coaching work is full of experimentation, both for himself and the client. He is always asking questions: "What happens when you do...?", "What happens if...?" As far as Richard Bandler is concerned, the techniques of NLP are a byproduct of the spirit of NLP. It is that wanton experimentation which creates the client change; the technique is simply a record of what happened during any particular session. We invite you to take the same attitude toward learning the Swish Pattern (or re-experiencing it in a new way, if you already know it). This means taking the technique out of the book and into your practice. The Swish Pattern is only alive in the space between coach and client, hypnotist and subject—not on the pages of this or any other book.

What is the Swish Pattern?

Put most simply, the Swish uses a change in one or more submodalities (the qualities of a mental picture, such as size or location) to link two visual representations, two pictures, together. The first picture is typically something seen in the outside world and it is a trigger for unwanted behavior. The second picture is imagined, and it represents the client at his or her best. We will address how we construct these images later in the book. The Swish links the two pictures together using a number of techniques: the first picture might get smaller as the second gets larger, or the first picture moves away as the second one moves closer. Again, we'll explore this in more detail later on.

The Swish Pattern is often used to deal with habits and compulsions. For example, if a person is a smoker, and wants to become a non-smoker, then the Swish might be used to help that person quit. Crucially, it is the client's problem—the urge to smoke—that is used to create the solution. But the Swish can also be used in a much more general way to install a new self-image, a new sense of self, in the client. As such, it can be extremely generative, meaning it can lead to positive changes in the client's life beyond merely stopping smoking.

The Swish installs the client's new self-identity using visual representations and submodalities. Visual representations are simply the pictures that we make inside our own minds. For example, if I were to think of a horse, I might see a picture of a cowboy on a horse, or a horse pulling a carriage, or a horse in a field. But I will see *some* kind of picture of a horse.

The submodalities of the visual representation refer to the way in which I hold this picture in my mind. For example, is the picture in color or black and white? Is it close to me, or far away? Is it large or small? Submodalities are used by the unconscious mind to code information about the meaning of the picture, and changing submodalities can have a huge impact on how we feel about the content of our internal visual representations. Images that are large, close to us, and in color tend to have more emotional content than images that are small, far away, and in black and white. The Swish takes advantage of natural mental processes such as this.

We will be going through the Swish in great detail later in the book, but to begin getting your mind in the right place, try this exercise:

Think of something that you would like to change in your life. It could be a feeling, a behavior, or a situation. You might have something in mind already, but if you don't, allow the information to come forward. Consider where you will be, physically, when this feeling, behavior, or situation next arises. Picture that place and take your time to visually recreate it in your mind. When you have identified that place, consider what you will be seeing immediately before you behave in the old, unresourceful way. What is it that you will be seeing in the outside world that will trigger your behavior?

Now, if you could be any way that you want to be, and if you could feel any way you want to feel, how would that be? Would you feel confident? Would you feel excited? Would you feel playful? And if you could picture yourself feeling this way—confident, excited, playful, or however you're feeling—what does this new you look like?

Now the pattern is in place. You have the trigger that you see immediately before you engage in the new behavior, and you have this new image of yourself.

It's that simple. It's a pattern, and with a little practice you will be able to "swish" between the two. A little repetition is key, so let me say that again: you have a trigger that you see immediately before you engage in the new behavior, and you have the new self-image.

One more time: you have the trigger... and a new self-image.

The trigger... new self-image.

Trigger... self-image.

This is the Swish in microcosm! Don't worry if it seems confusing at first; we will explain each step in detail in the following chapters.

Overview of this Book

The first few chapters of the book introduce you to the Swish. These chapters will help get your unconscious mind comfortable with learning the pattern before your conscious mind begins the actual learning.

Then we will look at the Swish in detail. We will break it down, step by step, then reassemble the whole thing into the wonderful pattern that is the Swish.

After that, we will look at some variations on the Swish such as the Hypnotic Swish, the Conversational Swish, and the Swish for Self-Coaching. We will also look at the New Behavior Generator Swish, the Swish as a recovery strategy, and for those who are feeling more active, the Physical Swish.

Finally, we will look at how the Swish can be used to help with specific problems such as smoking, nail biting, and dealing with difficult people.

Feel free to read the book from cover to cover or to dip in to it for specific techniques. For those unfamiliar with the Swish, or those who need to brush up their knowledge, we strongly suggest you read section two to give you a firm foundation in using this amazing pattern.

The History of the Swish Pattern

After reading the title of this chapter, you're probably asking yourself: "Why are they doing this? Why do I want to know the history of the Swish Pattern?" Those are really good questions to ask—it's good to be curious about why you're doing something. We encourage you to maintain that state of curiosity as you read the rest of the book. And here's why the history is important: the Swish is a perfect microcosm of NLP. It incorporates the fundamental building blocks of our mental world: internal representations and submodalities. It's a pattern that leads toward potentially massive generative change.

If you understand the Swish within the historical context of NLP, then you will understand the two main schools of NLP: those following the route of Richard Bandler and those following the route of John Grinder, and you will understand how every other school of NLP fits within the NLP landscape. In doing so you will begin to understand how the Swish can be used to both rewire the brain at the most fundamental level of sensory experience and install a new sense of self at the highest level of cognitive abstraction.

The Two Geniuses of NLP

In the early 1970s, Richard Bandler and John Grinder jointly developed the field of NLP. Bandler was a student at the University of Santa Cruz and John Grinder was a professor. Bandler had a genius for being able to instinctively model those around him, including the therapists he delighted in working with. Grinder was a trained linguist and was able to dissect what Bandler was doing and translate it into an explicit model that others could follow. Bandler and Grinder eventually disagreed about the direction that NLP should take, and each of them began to develop his own version or school of NLP to rectify what he saw as the shortcomings of the original system.

Grinder essentially worships the unconscious genius. He believes that each of us contains a unique personal genius and the aim of change work is to create a context in which this genius can arise. You can see this approach if you go to his trainings or study New Code NLP, which he developed.

Richard Bandler believes that experience is something that is constructed from smaller parts, and that the most effective way to create change is to first break the experience down into those parts, then change the parts — or change the sequence in which the parts arise. By doing so, you reconstruct the client's map and change the behavior. Bandler calls this Design Human Engineering (DHE); he sees himself, perhaps, as an engineer who is building a person from parts.

It's very important to understand these two approaches (in NLP in particular, and in change work in general) because they both work, and the truth has to include both of them.

Grinder and New Code NLP

Our interpretation of Grinder's approach is that he first creates the context for self-growth and change, then triggers the desire for such change and allows the change to happen. He discusses his principles at some length in his 1987 book, Turtles *All The Way Down*, written with Judith DeLozier. In this book, Grinder made the distinction between first-attention and second-attention, concepts that he borrowed from Peruvian-American author and anthropologist Carlos Castaneda. Castaneda describes first attention as "...animal awareness, which ... takes care of the day-to-day world in all its innumerable aspects. In other words, everything that one can think about is part of the first attention." Grinder talks about first attention in terms of internal representations and submodalities (internal pictures, sounds, and feelings, plus the qualities of those images, sounds, and feelings). Castaneda goes on to describe second attention as "...a more complex and specialized state of the global awareness [which has to do] with the unknown." Castaneda calls first-attention "right-side awareness" and second-attention "left-side awareness." In other words — and grossly simplifying — first-attention is the conscious mind and second-attention is the unconscious mind. As soon as we try to make something conscious, it becomes merely first-attention. According to Grinder, personal excellence lies in the field of not knowing. The more you try to "know," the further you move from your personal genius.

Bandler and Design Human Engineering

Our interpretation of Bandler's approach is that he uses the detail and sequencing of sensory experience, including internal senses such as the pictures you make in your mind, to construct a better reality. He has moved from traditional NLP to the idea of Design Human Engineering, although most DHE tools are similar to those that are used in traditional NLP.

The principal differences between Bandler and Grinder appear to be that Grinder, in New Code NLP, uses NLP for generative change (rather than simply to fix problems), and that Bandler, in Design Human Engineering, disavows eliciting information sequentially and embraces accessing it simultaneously. (By the way, both Ericksonian hypnosis and neuroscience view simultaneous processing as being a right brain and therefore unconscious mind activity.) In the end, Bandler and Grinder arrive in much the same place although they take very different routes.

The Swish Pattern in a Historical Context

So how does the Swish fit into this? As far as we know, the Swish is first discussed in Bandler's book, *Using Your Brain for a Change*. This book was published in 1985, ten years after Bandler and Grinder wrote their first book together, *The Structure of Magic*. *Using Your Brain for a Change* was the first book that discussed submodalities in detail and how the submodalities could be used in change work. The Swish is specifically described as a "submodality pattern" in that book.

So the Swish was perhaps designed by Bandler (rather than Grinder), and when you read about it in *Using Your Brain for a Change*, you very much get the idea that it is all about creating specific changes using submodalities and nothing else. Using the Swish to create generative change—placing the client into a context that would allow for bigger, more all-encompassing change—is not discussed in detail. Although Bandler does say at the end of the chapter that "…the swish pattern… sets the person in a direction that is generative and evolutionary," when he discusses the Swish Pattern in detail he tells the story of a woman who complained of smoking; he very explicitly describes how he creates the picture for the new self-image as a person "politely enjoying other people smoking" because he "didn't want her to see herself sneering at smokers and making life miserable for them." In other words, he was very focused on making the specific change that she had asked for in a way that was pleasing to Bandler, rather than a change that would necessarily lead to further positive changes in her life.

As we see it, and as Bandler hints, the Swish Pattern is much more than remedial change work. The Swish is potentially extremely generative in nature and is ideal for creating a context in which personal genius—as described by Grinder—can arise. It specifically creates a new self-image and gives the client the opportunity to build any resources she wishes, including personal genius, into this self-image. Using the Swish in this way utilizes the best of both Bandler and Grinder. By taking the time to use submodalities and allow the client to build up a new self-image that includes all the aspects of personal genius that they would like to express in their life, the Swish not only creates laser-focused, specific change, but also offers the opportunity to take the change to a generative level.

As you are reading this book and imagining using the Swish with your clients, colleagues, and friends, paint a broad picture of how the client will be at the end of the session. Do not limit yourself to only changing habits; you can also open up the client's unconscious mind to all of the possibility and potential that they have as a human being. And when you are working with clients, do not allow them to settle for results that are just "okay." The real pleasure of working with the Swish Pattern is in sharing your clients' joy as they build amazing and exciting new self-images, trusting that those self-images will create the contexts in which they can experience amazing changes in their lives.

When you imagine looking at a client's face and posture as he or she describes a problem, imagine being the sort of coach who can not only lead them to the solution they seek, but can also show them everything that they can be. When you see yourself as that sort of coach, your enthusiasm and fun will communicate itself to your client and you will both find yourselves moving into a bright future.

A Brief Example of the Swish Pattern

Before describing the Classical Swish Pattern in detail, we will provide you with a client example as an overview of how it might be used in practice. By Classical Swish we mean the Swish Pattern as taught in most mainstream NLP courses, as opposed to the alternative approaches we describe later in the book. As you listen to the dialogue between Janet and her coach unfolding, you can begin to imagine how effective you will be when you have the Swish Pattern embedded deeply inside your own abilities as a coach.

Janet is a smoker who wishes to become a non-smoker. The transcript below is only a part of the change work that was done with Janet.

Coach: So, Janet, you want to become a non-smoker?

Janet: Yes.

Coach: And why do you want to make this change?

Janet: It just annoys me that cigarettes have this hold over me. I have control over other areas of my life, but the cigarettes seem to have control over me. I don't like it.

Janet has just told us that smoking cigarettes is not aligned with her self-image. She is annoyed that cigarettes have a hold over her. This annoyance reflects the fact that she sees herself as somebody who is in control of her own life, but in the area of smoking she is clearly not in control. This context is absolutely ideal for the Swish because running the pattern will give her a very clear new self-image to which she will be drawn. The energy of this self-image will provide her with the energy to become a non-smoker.

Coach: I wouldn't like that either. I'm sure you want to feel in control of what you put inside yourself. I see that you brought your cigarettes along – what brand are they?

Janet: Marlboro.

Coach: Is that the brand that you normally smoke?

Janet: Yes.

For a smoker, the packet of cigarettes often provides a strong visual cue that precedes the behavior. The smoker sees the pack of cigarettes and it triggers the desire to smoke; the cigarette pack becomes an "anchor" for the smoking behavior. Smokers become very attached to their specific brand of cigarettes, and to the packaging of that brand. We will be using this visual representation of the pack of cigarettes later in the pattern.

Coach: Can you tell me about the times and places when you typically smoke over the course of the day?

Janet: Yes, I smoke first thing in the morning with my first coffee, then at work when I get bored. I have a cigarette at lunchtime, and usually after dinner.

Coach: So let's take one of those occasions. Let's take the cigarette that you have in the morning. Where are you when you smoke that?

Janet: On my front porch.

We are finding out when she smokes, the sorts of things that trigger her to smoke, where she is when she smokes, and how she feels when she has smoked. All this information may or may not be used in the Swish Pattern itself but will be useful in helping her to kick the habit.

For smokers, each cigarette can represent a separate problem. The cigarettes they smoke when they are stressed or bored at work may be very different from the cigarettes they smoke when they are with their friends in the evening. The cigarette in the daytime is triggered by stress or boredom and is smoked in the context of the office. It leads, perhaps, to a sense of focus, and allows the smoker to go back to her daily routine. The cigarette smoked in the evening perhaps is triggered by a sense of camaraderie with friends and allows her to relax. The hypnotist or coach should be aware of these differences and ensure that each and every cigarette that the client smokes is dealt with before considering the change complete. Here, the coach selects one of the cigarettes, the cigarette smoked in the morning, to begin work. Later in the session, the rest of the occasions on which Janet smokes will be dealt with. This transcript only deals with the first of the cigarettes. You will notice that there's a lot of repetition in this transcript. That's intentional. The repetition of key words by the coach keeps the ideas and images present in the region of Janet's brain called the "working memory" (the area you use when you "play a movie" in your mind). The coach needs to do this for long enough for the change to become hard-wired into the neurons of her brain.

Coach: So you're on your front porch. Why do you smoke then?

Janet: I guess it wakes me up.

Coach: And when you're on your front porch, what do you see when you're on your front porch?

Janet: I can see the streets, the tree in my front yard and my neighbor's car.

Coach: And as you are on your front porch what do you see immediately before you smoke?

Janet: I can see my cigarettes, the pack.

Coach: So you see the pack of cigarettes and you feel it is time to smoke?

Here we are gathering some more information about Janet's smoking, including the physical context in which she smokes (the environment, and what she sees there), and the purpose for smoking (which is to wake her up).

Coach: So what I would like you to do is pick up your packet of cigarettes. As you look at the packet of cigarettes, what do you notice about the pack? What catches your attention about the design?

Janet: I notice the gold foil on the front of the pack.

Coach: You notice the gold foil on the pack. And as you look at the gold foil on the pack I would like you to pick someplace within that gold foil on the pack.

Janet: The lion and the unicorn. They have a shield between them. That's what catches my attention.

Coach: Okay, so put the pack down for now.

The client has now got a visual representation of the pack of cigarettes, and also a particular visual point within the pack of cigarettes. This visual representation, the gold lion and unicorn around the shield, will be used as the "trigger picture" in the first half of the Swish Pattern. The trigger picture is what the client sees right before she engages in the unwanted behavior. We will discuss the trigger picture in detail in Chapter Five.

Coach: Now tell me again, why do you want to quit?

Janet: Because I feel awful. I just want to be free of the cigarettes.

Coach: And when you are living free of the cigarettes, living free as a healthy non-smoker, how will you be then as a person?

Janet: I won't have to hide my cigarettes! I'll be able to breathe easily. Actually, I've been thinking of running a marathon, so I guess I'll be a marathon runner!

Coach: You'll be free and you'll be able to breathe easily. You'll be running a marathon! So, Janet, what I would like you to do now is to make the picture of yourself being free. If you could see yourself living free, and breathing easily as a healthy non-smoker what would that be like?

Janet: I see myself running in a marathon!

Coach: You see yourself running in a marathon! And when you see yourself running in a marathon, when you look at yourself, what lets you know that you're free and that you can breathe easily as a healthy non-smoker?

Janet: I look healthy and strong and I'm smiling!

Coach: That's right, you look healthy and strong and you're smiling. You're free and you can breathe easily as a healthy non-smoker. And this question may sound a little silly, but when you see yourself healthy and strong, smiling, are you awake? By this I mean are you completely, tinglingly, alert and awake?

Janet: Yes!

This final question was designed to make sure that we captured the intention of the first cigarette of the day that Janet gave us earlier on, namely to wake up. We have now constructed a new image, called the outcome image. This outcome image is a picture of Janet herself. This is very important: the first picture is what she sees out of her own eyes immediately before she engages in the behavior. The second image is a picture of her as she wants to be. In NLP terms we say the first picture is associated and the second picture is dissociated.

Coach: So let's take that picture of you in the marathon, looking healthy and strong and smiling. I'd like you to take that picture and make it very small and embed it in the middle of the shield between the lion and the unicorn on the pack of cigarettes, right there. Can you do that for me?

Janet: Yes.

Coach: So in a moment—but not yet—I'm going to ask you to do the following: I'm going to ask you to look at the cigarettes and notice the gold foil and the lion and the unicorn and the shield between them. Notice that in the center of the shield is that small picture of you looking healthy and strong and smiling, running in the marathon. And when I tell you—but not before—I want you to imagine that picture of you, healthy and strong and smiling, running in the marathon, getting very big, life-size, bigger than life, so it totally covers the pack of cigarettes. Got it? The picture of you, healthy and strong and smiling, running in the marathon, just bursting out of the shield.

Janet nods. She is clearly following along. Explaining the technique in such detail while instructing her not to actually do it allows her unconscious mind to run the pattern before her conscious mind does. We are also chaining the two pictures together so that when she sees the pack of cigarettes in real life, her mind will automatically bring up the picture of the new person she wants to be. It is this chaining of representations that makes the Swish Pattern so powerful.

Coach: So see the pack of cigarettes. Now see that tiny picture of yourself right in the middle of the shield. Now the picture of you, strong and healthy and smiling, bursts out and appears right there in front of you, life-sized.

Janet's head moves back as the new picture leaps into place. This shows that she is following along with the pattern inside her mind. We are now going to repeat the pattern a few times in order to condition it but before we run the Swish again, it is important that we blank the screen. This is because we want to run the pattern from "seeing the packet of cigarettes" to "seeing the picture of herself as she wants to be" but not the other way around. We do not want her to think about the way she wants to be and then see a pack of cigarettes!

Coach: Okay, we are going to do that again. First, blank the screen. Now see that pack of cigarettes, see the lion and the unicorn with a shield in between them, and see that tiny picture of you, healthy and strong and smiling, in the center of the shield. Now—1, 2, 3—the picture of you, strong and healthy and smiling, bursting out. Now blank the screen. One more time—1, 2, 3—the picture of you, strong and healthy and smiling, right there in front of you.

Using the count of 1-2-3 allows the client time to mentally prepare by setting up the pictures in her mind, so the Swish happens easily. This is repeated two more times. The client is then instructed to run the pattern inside her own mind. We are watching to see her unconscious responses as she does this.

Coach: How was that?

Janet: That was amazing!

Coach: Pick up your pack of cigarettes. Take one out.

The client picks up the pack and opens it. Her hand reaches for a cigarette and then she stops.

Janet: I feel my ... my feelings for them have changed, I don't...

Almost all our smoking clients leave the office as non-smokers after one session, as did Janet. The Swish is one of several NLP patterns that we use, along with trance work, to help our clients to change. (Our complete stop-smoking protocol is laid out in our eBook *Quit: The Hypnotist's*

Handbook to Running Effective Stop Smoking Sessions, available at amazon.com.)

So, to summarize: the basic Swish Pattern simply involves asking the client to create two pictures. One picture will be what they actually see immediately before they engage in the behavior that they want to change. This is called the trigger picture (the pack of cigarettes in the example above). The second picture is the client as she wants to be. In the example above, it's the client, looking healthy and strong and smiling, in the marathon. We want this picture to have details that let her know that she has changed. In this case, the client in the picture is able to breathe easily, looks healthy and strong, and is smiling. The picture must be attractive to the client. Once we have these two images we can simply exchange the first picture for the second one.

Don't worry if you didn't get all of the pattern — we will be exploring it in more depth as we continue on in this book. For now just be aware that we are constructing a trigger picture and an outcome picture, and we are seeing them in sequence: trigger > outcome. If you understand this, you have the basic outline of the Swish. Furthermore, by reading the example above, your unconscious mind has already begun to assimilate and internalize the pattern. This will pave the way for your conscious understanding as you move through the book.

Now that we have laid the foundations of the Swish — but before we get into the nitty-gritty — we're going to explain how the Swish works on a neurological level. Understanding the effect that the Swish has on the neurological structure of the brain will enable you to understand why we do the steps in the order that we do them.

How the Swish Pattern Works

The question we are exploring in this chapter is: how does the Swish Pattern change the wiring of our brain to give us new and better choices of feeling and behavior?

The human brain is essentially a machine for "chaining representations." Our brains work by wiring one neuron or network of neurons to another. When the first neuron fires it sends a signal to the second neuron that tells it to fire (or sometimes *not* to fire). As neurons fire together, they begin to wire together, and by doing so they create the great levels of complexity and abstraction of the human mind. However, it all begins with one neuron firing and causing a second neuron to fire: links in a chain. Learning is the process whereby one set of neurons creates links to another set of neurons.

The Swish Pattern builds up a specific set of links between two specific sets of neurons. These new links will be automatically triggered when the client sees an object in the outside world. The client will then have a new internal experience that provides new choices. As we wire in this new response, the old response will cease and the old neural pathways, which are no longer useful, stop firing. Think about the new neural pathways that are being built as you read through the Swish Pattern, and follow along with the examples.

Let's try a little experiment. Think of something that you like to eat, and notice how you feel. Chances are you'll start to feel pretty good, and maybe pretty hungry. Now slow the process down. Imagine the food that you like to eat and notice what happens inside your mind. If necessary, slow it down even more. If you slow the experience down sufficiently, you'll find that you're making a picture or a movie inside your mind, some kind of image of you eating the food, perhaps. Perhaps you even begin to feel the texture of the food in your mouth, or its taste or smell. This is how you make yourself feel good.

Each step in this process becomes a link in a chain: see food > make picture of me eating food > feel hungry/good > eat food > feel full/good.

Other times you may overeat, so you see food, make a picture of yourself eating the food, feel good, actually eat the food, and then...feel bad. This is an unsuccessful strategy but it happens because you don't notice the final link in the chain (the feeling bad). Think about the last time you overate or overindulged in some other way. Go back to the point in time immediately before you took the first mouthful. What is going on inside your mind? Are you seeing the food, making a picture or movie of you eating food, and getting that good feeling? Now try including the final links of the chain: see the food > make a picture inside of you eating the food > feel good > make a picture of yourself stuffed and bloated > feel bad. Now you'll probably be less likely to overeat!

The more times we do something, the stronger the corresponding neural pathways become. At some point they become habitual. The representations (pictures, feelings, and self-talk) are chained together so strongly that the behavior becomes automatic. The representations are still there, but they have dropped out of our conscious awareness. Think about brushing your teeth: There are several steps to the process, but your brain has made them automatic. Once you pick up the toothbrush, all the rest is done on autopilot. We do the behavior without really being aware that we are doing it.

The brain does this on purpose because automatic processes are very efficient, and the brain loves efficiency. It takes much less energy for our brains to do things on autopilot than to have to think about them. However, when our brain has constructed a bad strategy, and that strategy has gone onto autopilot, then we can be in a lot of trouble. Bad strategies running on autopilot are the reasons for most of our problems.

The Swish Pattern takes advantage of the brain's tendency to automate strategies. The Swish uses a conscious process to chain two visual representations together, but the way we do the Swish involves the unconscious mind and therefore allows the process to become coded into your unconscious much more quickly than by going through a completely conscious or completely unconscious learning process. This is what makes patterns like the Swish different from cognitive and behavioral therapy, or CBT. In CBT, new thinking and behavioral chains are built, but there is less emphasis on bringing the unconscious mind into the process and it can therefore take a little time. Remember our discussion of Bandler and Grinder in Chapter Three? Grinder's criticism of classic NLP revolves around the fact that it was "first attention" (conscious mind), and failed to include "second attention" (unconscious mind). The Swish uses both. The client can follow along consciously while the unconscious mind is involved in building the outcome picture. Using submodalities to switch from one picture to another favors the unconscious mind, too. This is what makes the Swish effective. Used properly, it has elements of both first attention and second attention, of conscious processing and unconscious processing.

Let's consider the example we looked at earlier, the Swish used to stop smoking, and break it down in light of our new understanding. The first picture the client sees is the packet of cigarettes. With her old, automatic strategy, she might unconsciously imagine herself smoking one, and then begin to feel good. Then she actually smokes one. Then she may feel bad. She may even—eventually—die of something unpleasant, but she almost certainly did not picture those possibilities before she smoked. If she did, she would probably not smoke.

In the Swish, we are taking the first picture—what she sees outside of herself before she smokes—and we are attaching a new link in the chain. We are creating a new neural pathway from that picture. So the first link in the new chain is the same as the first link in the old, problem chain: the pack of cigarettes. But the second link of the new chain is now the outcome picture. We ask the client to think of how she *wants* to be: a healthy non-smoker, free of cigarettes. She creates another picture in her mind. We want her to see herself in the picture because we want her to think, "I want to be that person!" If she does not see herself in the picture, she may not have the desire to become that person because she might feel like she already is her (even if she isn't yet). Without the emotional desire to become that person, there is no second attention, no unconscious involvement in the Swish, which may lead to it being ineffective.

So now we have the two pictures. We need to "chain" them together. We do this by seeing the first picture and then replacing it with the second picture, using a Swish. The manner of replacement is important, and we will talk about this later. We condition this chain using repetition, as well as the emotional involvement we have already mentioned. And, of course, we blank the screen in between each repetition, so that the chain only runs in one direction: picture one > picture two. It does *not* run: picture two > picture one. Neurological conditioning chains the images together and begins to create the effect that we want. The brain works through associations: we think of one thing and it makes us think of another thing, and that makes us feel a certain way. The client thought of her pack of cigarettes and her desire to smoke. Now she thinks of her pack of cigarettes, sees herself as she wants to be, and has the feeling of desire to be that new person, the person who is free from cigarettes. We have inserted an extra link in her chain of thought which is more powerful than the original desire.

Think of the Swish as a way to wire a new neural pathway from an image that used to trigger a problem to the new person that the client wants to be. This makes the steps of the Swish easy to understand. We suggest that you keep this metaphor of the new neural pathway in mind as you read this book. Reading the book is itself a process, and therefore it creates new neural pathways. If you become confused at any point you are in exactly the right place because confusion always precedes understanding. So if you feel confusion, simply picture all the new neural pathways that are being constructed in your mind.

The Swish Pattern in Detail

In this section, we will explain the steps of the Swish Pattern in detail; we'll also present some of the choices you have as a coach or practitioner. Finally, we will explore some of the things you need to watch out for when using the Swish Pattern with your clients.

Let's run through the basic steps one more time:

> 1) Get the context for the work by asking your client to think of a specific time and place where they engage in the problem behavior.
>
> 2) Elicit picture one, also known as the trigger picture, and the emotion connected with the image, by asking them what they see immediately before they engage in the problem behavior. They should not see themselves in this picture; rather, they should see what they see when they look out of their own eyes. In NLP terms, they should be "associated" into the picture.
>
> 3) Put the picture to one side for now. Give the client space to disengage from the problematic neural chain by distracting them in some way. This is called a "break state." This allows them a chance to begin building the new resourceful picture. It is much easier to go from a neutral to a positive state than it is to go from a negative to a positive state.
>
> 4) Elicit the outcome picture (picture two) by asking the client how they will be different—how they will be as a person—when they have made this change. Ask them to make a picture of

themselves as they will be in the future. Make this picture attractive—super attractive! They should see themselves in this picture, so they are not looking out of their own eyes, but looking *at* themselves, as if looking at a photograph or a frame from a movie. Seeing yourself in a picture or movie in your mind is called being "dissociated" in NLP.

5) Break state again by distracting them, perhaps asking them an irrelevant question such as "do you smell popcorn," or "what is your phone number backwards."

6) Do the Swish. Ask them to think of picture one, and then replace it with picture two. This is the Swish. The Swish should be an active process that involves the unconscious mind. We will discuss how to move one image and replace it with another in detail in Chapter Eight.

7) Repeat to condition. By repeating the Swish Pattern a number of times we strengthen ("condition") the new neural pathways that are being built in the brain.

8) Test.

Coaching Context and Pre-Frames

Before you can begin the Swish Pattern, or even decide what type of Swish Pattern to use, you must first consider the context. You also need to "set up" the work you are about to do with the client so that you can be sure that the process will be successful and run smoothly. This set up is known as "framing" in NLP, and any framing that you do before the work starts is called a "pre-frame."

Any piece of coaching, or "change work" as it is called, takes place within a certain context. These could include:

1) Traditional NLP coaching.

2) Formal hypnosis.

3) Business coaching.

4) Informal coaching (for example, with a friend).

Of course, there are as many contexts for change work as there are people on the planet, but the above list includes the most common types of coaching. Once you have determined the context in which the coaching is to take place, you can decide what type of Swish Pattern to use. If you are doing NLP coaching, for example, you can use the classic NLP Swish Pattern. If you are doing more formal hypnosis, then the Swish Pattern may be more hypnotic. If you are doing business coaching, then the pattern may be more conversational. If you are simply speaking with a friend, then the pattern may be more conversational still. We will go through various versions of the Swish Pattern later in the book.

Is the Swish the Right Pattern to Use?

The Swish Pattern is particularly useful when a client engages in a problem behavior that is out of alignment with his or her self-image. In other words, the client does not see herself as the sort of person who engages in that behavior.

The Swish Pattern is also a fantastic general-purpose pattern because it is very generative. By "generative" we mean that it generates change at a high, abstract level: the level of identity, the level that is all about knowing who you truly are and who you wish to be. Ultimately, the Swish Pattern is not simply about changing a behavior; it is about moving the client toward a new, more positive and more resourceful self-image. Running the Swish Pattern with a client may result in changes that spread throughout her life, not simply in the behavior that she wanted to change. You, too, can use the Swish Pattern with your clients to create powerful generative change.

So now you understand the context of the coaching work, you have decided to use the Swish Pattern, and you have decided what sort of Swish Pattern to use: Classic, Hypnotic, or Conversational. You are almost ready.

Before you begin the pattern itself, you should set an appropriate context with the client. At a minimum, this will involve gaining rapport and compliance (which we will discuss further, below) and setting the expectation that change will occur. Depending upon the context in which the coaching takes place, it may also include an explanation of the coaching process, or of hypnosis. Let's look at each of these steps in more detail.

> 1) Obtaining compliance from the client. This will generally involve building rapport (a relationship of trust between coach and client) and then testing it by asking the clients to complete certain tasks. For example, we can ask the client to sit in a certain chair, put their feet flat on the floor, and so on.
>
> 2) Setting the expectation that the Swish Pattern will result in change. Depending upon the client, this may involve explaining how the brain chains images together, as described above, and that we will be using this natural process to help the client get what they want out of the session. In addition, it may involve telling them the story about another client who used the Swish to achieve some amazing change.

Finding the Problem Context and the Trigger

The first step in the Swish Pattern is to find the trigger picture.

The trigger picture is typically what the client sees in the outside world immediately before they have the problem. Examples might be a pack of cigarettes (if they are a smoker), a small imperfection on the fingernail (if they are a nail-biter), or some junk food (if they have unhealthy eating habits). In order to find the trigger picture, you first have to find the context in which the problem arises. Bear in mind that there may be several such contexts for any one problem, and that you may need to run the Swish Pattern separately on each of these contexts, even if the outcome picture is the same (although, at some point, the change will generalize across all contexts).

Finding the Context of the Problem Behavior

All behaviors take place in a specific context. This context may be a place, an activity, a social setting, another person, or even another behavior. It may be a group of people with whom the behavior takes place. It is important, for all sorts of reasons, for us to understand the context of a behavior. When it comes to the Swish Pattern, the context is important because you need to be able to associate the client into their behavior. If you do not do this successfully, you may not get the correct trigger picture.

And how do you know if you have been successful? Look at the client's reaction when they see the trigger. Their posture may change, their facial expression may change, and their breathing may change.

It will be more difficult to test your work if you do not have the correct context. You will also not be able to do a "future pace" (a mental rehearsal of the next time the client will be in the situation where they want the new behavior) if you do not have the correct context. So getting that context, with as much specificity as possible, is really important.

Let's revisit, once more, the example of the client who came in to stop smoking. When specifically does the client smoke a cigarette? The more precisely you can answer this, the easier the change work becomes. It is much easier to run the Swish on a specific cigarette that the client smoked at 8:30 in the morning on Thursday than on every cigarette she has ever smoked in her life. Some people think that it would be easier to take all the client's experiences and change them all at the same time. After all, if you only change the client's experience of the cigarette that they smoked on Thursday at 8:30, then won't every other cigarette they smoked still be a problem for them? The answer is no. As you begin to repeat the pattern on various experiences and various cigarettes, the client's unconscious mind begins to generalize the change. The human brain likes to categorize things by grouping similar experiences together. So, for example, the brain may link all the cigarettes that are smoked first thing in the morning as one set of experiences, and the cigarettes that are smoked after dinner as a totally different set of experiences. Or the client's unconscious may view the evening cigarette as being the same as the cigarettes she smoked in the morning. In any case, the mind will categorize the experiences into groups, and you must deal with each group in order to create lasting change.

So how do you associate the client into a particular experience? It's simple: First, you ask them for a specific time and place in which they engaged in the behavior. You may have a client who says, "I do this all the time," or, "It happens all the time." If they say this, you can respond: "In that case, it should be easy to pick one of those times." It is worth repeating that the more specifically you elicit the time and the place in which the event took place, the easier the change work will be. If your client gives you a list of times and places, (as in the cigarette example), make a note of them all. You may have to visit each and every one of those contexts to make sure that your change work has generalized.

Once the client has chosen a specific event at a specific time and place, then you can begin to associate them. You can say: "So it happened on Thursday. Where are you?" Note that shift into the present tense—"Where are you?"—even though you are talking about events that took place in the past. Using the present tense will take the client back to that time and place and reassociate them. It will become the present, the "now." Next, you ask them about their sensory experience: "What are you seeing? What are you hearing? What are you feeling?" Notice again that you do not ask them what they *saw*; you ask them what they are *seeing*, for the same reasons: because it helps associate them into the experience. This associated context forms the foundation within which the Swish will take place.

Finding the Trigger Picture

Once you have identified the context, you can begin to search for the trigger picture. This is what the client sees in the outside world immediately before he or she engages in the problem behavior. In the example above, it is the pack of cigarettes. With a nail-biter, it might be a small nick or imperfection in the nail that "needs" to be bitten off. In order to do the Swish accurately and effectively, you need the correct trigger picture.

Sometimes the trigger picture will not be easy to find. For example, a client might seek help because he habitually gets angry with his spouse, but not all the time. So it is not his spouse who triggers the anger; it is something more specific. It might be something that his spouse says, or a facial expression that his spouse has, or something similar. If you do not use the correct picture, then you will not be attaching the outcome picture to the correct trigger. You might not be lighting up the correct neural network, and the change work might not be so effective.

So how do you make sure that you have enough information about the trigger picture to allow you to do the Swish Pattern? You should ask for some specific, small detail. When you have that, then you will know that the client is paying attention to the trigger. For example, for the client who gets angry with his spouse, let's say he tells you that it happened on Monday, in the evening, in the kitchen. You begin to associate him into the event and run him through the experience based upon what he tells you—not your own mind reading. You repeat back the information he gives you and watch for changes in his body language and facial expression: "So it's Monday evening; you're in the kitchen; your wife walks in, and she asks you how your day has been. You look at her, and you see that expression on her face: You see her lips are turned down..." As you say this, the client's posture and facial expression begin to show signs of anger. So, in this case, the trigger picture is clearly his wife with her lips turned down.

There are two keys to finding the trigger picture. The first is patience and persistence. You need to keep asking questions, and make sure the client is associated into the experience, in a specific context, until you come to the moment when the client loses conscious control. For example, the client's conscious mind is telling her not to smoke, but she unconsciously reaches for cigarettes anyway. If you miss the moment, or if you are not sure what that moment is, you can always go back to the beginning and walk them through the experience again.

The second key to finding the correct trigger is noticing when the client changes his or her state. At the moment the client sees the trigger picture, an automatic and unconscious process begins to run. As this process runs unconsciously, her internal state will change. This change might be reflected in her posture, breathing, skin color, voice tone, facial expression, or in other physical changes. In NLP we call these signs BMIRs — Behavioral Manifestations of Internal Representations.

The trigger causes the client to change their state. The combination of the trigger and the state it generates is called a "synesthesia," or a visual-kinesthetic synesthesia (because the visual picture creates a kinesthetic feeling), or simply a V-K synesthesia for short. What the client sees immediately before the synesthesia is the trigger picture. It is the trigger in the outside world that causes them to lose conscious control and then engage in the unwanted behavior. So the form of the synesthesia for an unwanted habit is "see the trigger" > "feel the desire." In the case of a smoker, the synesthesia might be "see the pack of cigarettes" > "want to smoke."

In the case of a smoker or a nail-biter, finding the synesthesia may be relatively easy. For example, in the case of the smoker, you may present them with their pack of cigarettes and watch their reaction. If they look like they

44

want to immediately reach forward and take one, then you have found at least one of their triggers. Similarly, if a nail-biter looks down at an imperfection on their nail and looks like they want to bite it, you probably found their trigger. Of course, there can be wide variety in triggers. A smoker may only smoke in a certain context, such as at work. If he sees the pack of cigarettes at any other time in the day, he does not want to smoke. Therefore there is something in the work environment that creates the desire to smoke; it's not just the pack of cigarettes by itself. In this case, if you simply did the Swish on the pack of cigarettes, then you would not have addressed the underlying cause of smoking, something that stresses him at work: perhaps a certain look on his boss's face, or seeing an email from a certain person.

This subtle point is very important for properly understanding and utilizing the Swish. In the example of the smoker, he is smoking at work because he is stressed. His boss told him off, and as soon as he got back to his desk he picked up his cigarettes and went outside to smoke. What is the trigger here? You could, of course, say that the trigger is the pack of cigarettes. This is what he sees immediately before he smokes, and when he decides he wants to smoke he probably pictures the pack of cigarettes or something similar. However, there is another synesthesia at work. This is the moment in time where he sees or hears his boss and feels stressed. So there are two very different synesthesias, each with different triggers and different resulting feelings. The first is "see boss" > "feel stress,", and the second is "see pack of cigarettes" > "feel desire." Which synesthesia should you work on? The answer is that you could work on either, and you should work with both. If you were able to remove all sources of stress from the client's life, then he may no longer smoke. If you remove the desire to smoke from the pack of cigarettes, he may continue to feel stressed but find some other way of dealing with it. So the better answer is to deal with both synesthesias. You can do a Swish on the pack of cigarettes and another Swish on his boss's face. (We discuss a Swish specifically designed to deal with difficult people later in the book.)

In summary, there may be several triggers for any issue. The coach should deal with as many of these as necessary to fully generalize the change work. If some important trigger is missed, then the problem may recur in that context.

Summary

In order to find the synesthesia, you need to:

>1) Find out in what context the client engages in the problem behavior. If the client is a smoker, maybe she smokes at breakfast time, at work, and in the evenings.
>
>2) Find a specific time and place in which the client engaged in the unwanted behavior. For example, she smoked at work yesterday.
>
>3) Associate the client back into that specific time and place.
>
>4) Guide the client to slow down the movie of that memory until she finds the exact synesthesia. You will know when that has happened because you will see the emotional reaction in the client.
>
>5) Once you have found the synesthesia, the visual part of it is the trigger picture. The more precisely you hone in on the trigger picture, the more precise the change work will be. We cannot stress this enough.

Doing a Break State

Once you have found the trigger picture at the point of synesthesia, you need to do a "break state."

A break state is an NLP technique that is generally used to move the client from a negative state into a neutral or more positive one. It doesn't matter too much what the neutral or positive state is; you simply want the client out of the negative state. The break state is useful if you are about to ask the client about a more resourceful state. It may be difficult for her to find a resourceful state if she is feeling negative—it's easier to move the client into a neutral state first.

The break state is an important step in the Swish because, when a client is in a problem state, it is difficult to activate the new neural pathways she will use in creating the positive image of the outcome. Think of it this way: When you are feeling down or depressed, and some kind soul tells you to "cheer up," it's difficult to do because the shift in state is so great. By breaking the state, you have a neutral starting point from which to build the positive outcome.

To break state for a client engaged in the Swish, you need to dissociate them from the first picture so that the neural pathways associated with the problem are no longer active. The client is then free to create the second picture, which is connected with a resourceful state. There are several ways of achieving the break state. The coach could suggest that the client blank their internal screen, wiping out their trigger picture. A more natural and conversational way is to ask them a question completely unrelated to both the problem and the resource. For example, the coach could ask about the client's evening plans, or perhaps a pleasant vacation they had. This jump in topic will create a very brief moment of confusion, which pulls the client's attention away from the picture associated with the problem behavior and changes their state. Once the state has changed then the client is ready to begin creating a new picture, one that will be connected with their desired outcome: a more resourceful state.

When you do the break state you are looking for the client's BMIRs to change as a way of verifying that his state has also changed. You might see a shift in physiology, or a color change in his face. If he still looks like he is in a negative state, then you may have to do another break state. Once you notice a change in his state to either a neutral or a positive state, then you can move ahead and create the outcome image, which we discuss below.

Creating the New Self-Image

In this chapter we will talk about the second important piece of the Swish Pattern: creating the new self-image.

As we have discussed before, the Swish works by linking what you actually see to a new internal image of how you want to be as a person. This is what makes the Swish Pattern generative: the new self-image creates a context in which amazing change can happen. For this reason, we are going to go into detail about the various ways in which we can generate this new self-image. Investing time in creating a powerful new self-image for use in the Swish Pattern is time well spent.

What qualities will the new self-image have? The image will have certain qualities, some of which we have already discussed: The image will be dissociated. This means that your client will see herself in the picture as if she were looking at herself in a photograph. The image should start out small, say about the size of a postage stamp or smaller, and then expand to life-size. The expanded image will have positive submodalities, which typically means that it will be bright, colorful, and three-dimensional.

How different will the new self-image be from the way the client is now? This depends upon what the client is trying to achieve, as well as her preferences and your preferences as the coach. Some coaches will keep things simple and help the client to construct a self-image of some simple but different behavior. Some coaches will construct a more compelling self-image with additional capabilities, while others will construct an idealized self-image including beliefs, values, and self-identity. Here we will give examples of the range of self-images that could be constructed for a client who bites his nails.

Creating a Simple Self-Image

It is possible to run the Swish Pattern with a very simple outcome picture, a picture in which the client is doing something—anything—other than the problem behavior. For example, if you are running the Swish Pattern for a nail-biter, then the outcome picture could simply be the nail-biter more-or-less as he is now, but doing something other than biting his nails (which of course means that he has better-looking nails). It is perfectly possible that the idea of having nice-looking nails would motivate the client to stop biting his nails. During the Swish, the coach helps the client's unconscious mind to realize that changing the behavior (nail-biting) will lead to a change in appearance (nicer nails). Rather than simply looking at his chewed nails and thinking, "I wish I didn't bite my nails," the client's mind now has a new path to follow: "Keep your fingernails out of your mouth and have nice-looking nails."

The problem with this approach, if there is one, is that it does nothing to address the root causes of the nail-biting. The client is biting his nails for some purpose, to satisfy some secondary gain. ("Secondary gain" refers to the underlying psychological cause of the behavior: the hidden benefit to the client.) Therefore, the next step in building the self-image will address that.

Adding New Capabilities to the Self-Image

By adding additional capabilities to the new self-image, the Swish becomes even more generative, as it can address the underlying causes of the problem.

In the case of the nail-biter, the new self-image might be him with nice, neat, clean fingernails, together with some new resource, capability, or skill, such as self-control. Self-control becomes the resource that he needs in order to make the change. When the Swish is installed, the next time he looks at his fingernails and sees a snag that might have previously caused him to bite, he now sees the outcome picture, which includes both the self-control and the positive consequences of having that self-control: nice fingernails. Even though the image is dissociated, by seeing it he will realize that self-control is something he desires, and therefore his unconscious mind will make it available.

Adding New Beliefs and Values to the Self-Image

You can continue to build an image using beliefs, values, identity, and even values beyond identity. So the self-image could include:

The *values* that are being satisfied by the change in the behavior. What is important to the client about not biting his nails? More to the point, what is important to him about being a person with clean, fresh, unbitten nails?

Beliefs. What does he believe about himself as he explores the world with his new, clean, unbitten nails?

Identity. Who is he as a person — what is his identity — after the change? How does changing this one behavior make him part of something bigger?

Beyond identity. What larger plan is he satisfying by changing his behavior? Perhaps he is setting a good example for his children? Perhaps he is treating his body with the respect it deserves? Perhaps it is God's plan for him?

As you can see, there are many new levels, capabilities, values, and beliefs that can be built into the new self-image. For each, the coach should ask the client what he sees, specifically, in the picture of his new self that lets him know that the quality he desires is present. It could be the posture, the breathing, the facial expression, whatever he identifies. It's important to make a link between specific qualities in the picture and the values, capabilities, and beliefs that the client wants.

Asking lots of questions will help the client to create a picture of how he will be and who he will be as a person once he has achieved his goal. This is the fun part of the Swish Pattern, because the client gets to dream and play. If the client is not having fun in this step, then the coach is doing it wrong! The client must be attracted to the new image so that it can pull him in a new direction. We are essentially saying to the mind: "Not that, but this." See the fingernail, and your mind immediately creates the outcome image and says: "Not 'Biting that finger nail,' but 'This person I want to be.'"

Eliciting a strong desire for the new self is a crucial part of successfully leading a client through the Swish. If the client does not truly desire the new self, the Swish will be only partly successful at best. The coach must use her own enthusiasm to create that desire in the client. To illustrate this, here is an excerpt from an NLP training course that the authors of this book ran recently. One of the students, Kristina, acting as coach, was saying that her client was not attracted to the outcome picture, and as a result the Swish "didn't work." Here Shawn explains to Kristina what she could have done differently while at the same time covertly running the Swish pattern to install a new level of "go-for-it" in her.

In order to demonstrate that it is the coach's state rather than the archetype or self-image that controls the process,

Shawn deliberately breaks all the rules by picking an archetype, NASCAR racer Danica Patrick, that Kristina didn't know and would normally have had no interest in.

The demonstration starts with Kristina's question:

Kristina: With the client, would you be asking them what else they wanted in the picture? I asked my client whether he wanted anything else in the picture, and he said no, it's fine. So I'm wondering if I went more into that, maybe he'd get more attached to the new self-image?

Shawn: One way of approaching it is to go with an archetype, a character from a book or from history, of somebody they know. Because that archetype is going to bring with it all sorts of positive things: an identity, beliefs and values, capabilities and resources, as well as behaviors. It's a package deal and it saves a lot of time. It may not be the perfect package, but it gets you a good package. And for most people the right archetype is going to automatically have some attraction.

Kristina: So, you mean a historical figure?

Shawn: Historical, fictional, mythical, biblical... NASCAR racer... What was that woman called? Danica Patrick...the first female NASCAR racer to have pole position at Daytona, the Super Bowl of NASCAR.

[Shawn is now going to elicit a strong positive state and attach it to a picture of Danica Patrick.]

And this woman has pole position! She's in number one position! Danica Patrick! Isn't that awesome! Isn't she self-actualizing as a woman! If you can imagine the qualities — you may not be into NASCAR, in fact I'm sure most the people in the room are not — but the quality she must have as an archetype, the raw courage that you need to have to drive that car around that narrow track at 200 miles an hour and you're just gunning that thing! Isn't that fucking incredible?! She's a woman, she doesn't have all that male testosterone stuff, but she has DRIVE, just pure "go for it" DRIVE. Now, isn't that something you could use more of?

[Shawn can see that Kristina is "lighting up" in a positive state whenever he says DRIVE. You will also see that Shawn has switched to using the pronoun "you," in order to lead Kristina to "become" Danica Patrick. Shawn now describes the trigger picture for Kristina—what she will see in the real world. In this case, it's an unenthusiastic client.]

And when you think of that time in your life when you would normally say to yourself [whiney voice] "I don't know if I can do this…" [Laughter]… and the thing you see when you look at your client, and you see they're not attaching to that image, and they say [whiney voice] "I don't think I'm attaching to this…."

[Kristina now has the outcome picture of Danica Patrick as an archetype, and the trigger picture of the unenthusiastic client. All that remains is to run the Swish.]

And suddenly a picture appears in your mind of Danica Patrick and you feel that DRIVE, that energy; there may be cars in front of you but you go, "I'm gunning it!!! I'm gunning it for that line!!!"

[Kristina is laughing and bouncing in her seat.]

And that's the Swish, are you getting some emotional attachment now? [Laughter.]

Kristina: Wow, and I didn't even know who she was!

Jess: And he got in touch with the energy of it and the passion of it. If he had just said, "Think of Danica Patrick… Swish!" [Laughter.] Instead, he got up out of his seat and embodied the energy of it, and that's the theater!

Shawn: I even picked the archetype there, and you don't even know who she is! [Pointing at Kristina.]

Kristina: I didn't, but I do now! [Laughter.]

When the client has created her new outcome image, she should literally be licking her lips in anticipation. It's your job as the coach to get her there!

We will now discuss various ways that you can create a new self-image for yourself, or help your clients to create theirs.

Consciously Building the Outcome Picture

The first and most obvious way to build an outcome picture is to ask the client. We can simply say: "Who will you be as a person when you've made this change? How will you be feeling? What skills and abilities will you have? With these new feelings, with these new skills and abilities, how will that new you look? How will she be different? What will you see that will let you know that this new you has these skills and abilities?"

In describing her new self in the outcome picture, the client may talk about the expression on her face. She may say, "I'll be smiling." She may talk about her breathing being deeper or easier. She may talk about her posture, about how she'll be standing straighter, or about being more relaxed. She may even talk about how she'll be dressed.

When we have this new picture, we can begin to enhance it by adding even more skills and abilities, beliefs and values. We can ask: "What else will you have when you've made this change? What other skills and abilities will you have? What else would you like to put into the picture? Remember you can have anything that you want!" When the client mentions a new skill or ability, or a new feeling, then the coach can begin to associate her into it — so that she feels it. Supposing the client says, "I will have a sense of confidence," but she doesn't yet look like she is feeling confident. Then you can say: "What's it like when you're feeling confident?" This has the added benefit of embedding the command: "You're feeling confident!" Encourage the client to add positive and fun resources into the picture so that, when she looks at it, she feels fantastic. She should think: "Yes, I want to be this person!" If she looks at the picture and she seems like she doesn't care about it, then you haven't yet done your job as a coach. Get your clients excited!

Unconsciously Building the Outcome Picture

A second way of creating the outcome picture is to rely on the unconscious mind. In order to do this you have to ask questions that either make no sense to the conscious mind, overwhelm the conscious mind's ability to answer, or both. Here's one example:

"Aside from the smoking, what is everything else about who you can be that you haven't been seeing until now?"

This question does several things:

It overwhelms the conscious mind by being a relatively complex three-part question, as well as by asking for "everything else."

It instructs the unconscious mind to search for something aside from the smoking, something different.

It invites the unconscious mind to make a picture of a new self-image—"who you can be," "haven't been seeing until now."

Typically, when you ask a question like this, the client will look momentarily confused, and perhaps move their eyes up and begin to look to left and right for an answer. You can help the client to find the outcome picture simply by holding your left hand up, palm towards your client, inviting them to look up and to their right. This will take them into the visual-create portion of their visual field; one way to make it easier to create new pictures in our minds (rather than memories of things we have seen) is to look up and to the right. Looking up takes our mind into a visualization mode, and to the right takes us into a mode of imagination.

If they can't find the new self-image—if they say something like, "I'm not sure"—you can help them by reminding them of why they want to make this change in their lives. Supposing they came in to stop smoking because they are concerned about their health and afraid they may not live to see their grandchildren graduate college. In doing the Swish Pattern, you ask them: "Aside from the smoking, what is everything else about who you can be that you haven't been seeing until now?" Your client looks up, glances left, glances right, looks at you a little confused and says, "I'm not sure." You smile at them, and you say: "That's right, you're not sure about that, but you are sure that you want to watch your grandchildren on graduation day, and as you're seeing them graduate, who are you as a person?" And you raise your left hand, palm towards them, leading them into their visual-create area.

So you are validating their response ("that's right, you're not sure"), reminding them of their value ("you want to watch your grandchildren on graduation day"), and using that value to help them find the new self-image ("as you're seeing them graduate, who are you as a person"), as you lead their gaze into visual-create.

Using this approach allows the new self-image to be built by their unconscious mind, and—because it's the unconscious mind that is driving the behavior—the new self-image generated by it is likely to be more effective.

Using Archetypes

Another way to generate the new picture is to use a mental image of somebody the client admires. It could be a picture of somebody he knows, somebody he has seen in a movie, somebody he imagines from a book, or perhaps a historical figure. These people will act as archetypes.

To help a client think creatively about whom he might want to model, it's good to offer him some ideas. For example, you may want to tell him how you used to imagine being a movie character:

"Personally, I always used to like to watch Batman on television. I would really get into the role of being Batman. I would stand like Batman; I would walk like Batman; I would even breathe like Batman. I would put on Batman's expression; I would speak like Batman, and deep down inside I would take on the beliefs and values of Batman. And when you do take on a role like that, you feel strong and confident. I told myself, "You can do anything! You can be who you want to be! You have all the power and resources you need!" I was a superhero! That's very exciting for a young child. My brother and I would spend our time fighting imaginary villains, but for us they were totally real. Children have great imaginations, and your imagination is a gift because it allows you to be anything you want to be and to do anything you want to do. So, ready to play?"

Telling this sort of story to your client will allow him to activate his imagination. You can then ask him, "Whom do you know—from movies, books, history, or even people you know in your life—who handles this sort of situation the way you would like to handle it?"

Give him enough time pick somebody whom he really admires. He'll tell you who this person is and what the characteristics of the person are. Perhaps the main characteristic is confidence. When he is describing this hero, this archetype, you want to see him go into a state of confidence. You can see this in action in the following excerpt from a client session.

Coach: So when you think of a person that you see in the movies, or a person you've read about in books—someone who has been able to handle this in the way you would like to handle it—who would that person be?

Client: Iron Man.

So now we have the character, the archetype.

Coach: Iron Man? I love Iron Man! And when you think of Iron Man, what characteristics does he have that would help him in this situation?

Client: Confidence and self-esteem.

What? Iron Man has confidence and self-esteem? This sounded to the coach like the conscious mind talking, because there was no emotional energy expressed in the words. He wanted to challenge this and get the unconscious mind involved.

Coach: Really? Confidence and self-esteem? What about his cool jet suit? What about his rockets?

Client: Oh yeah, those are totally cool! I love the way he flies around, and if anything gets in his way, he can just zap it!

Great! The client is finally having fun and his unconscious mind is involved. Now we have to turn Iron Man into something we can use in the session. We are going to ask about who Iron Man is—his beliefs and values—and go from there.

Coach: And when he's flying around in his jet suit and zapping things with his rockets, who is he then, as a person? What does he believe? What's important to him?

Client: He's just bad! He knows he's unstoppable, that he can do anything! I love the way he uses his mind as well to solve problems, to get what he wants.

Coach: That's right, he's just bad, he's unstoppable and he can do anything! And he uses his mind to solve problems, and to get what he wants. That's just awesome! And when you see him, what is it about him that lets you know he's so bad, that he's so unstoppable, that he can do anything?

Client: I guess it's the way he stands. He sort of has this posture where he leans forward and you know he's ready!

Coach: That's right, he does have that posture; he leans forward and you know he's ready for anything. He's unstoppable; he can do anything; he's just totally bad!

Client: Yeah!!

Now the coach returns to comment about using the mind to solve problems.

Coach: And when you see him, his posture—the way he leans forward so you know he is ready—what is it about him that lets you know that he can use his mind to solve any problem and get what he wants?

Client: It's the look on his face; it's determined but it's also thoughtful. You know that his mind is fully engaged.

Coach: That's right, it's the look on his face—determined and thoughtful—and you know his mind is fully engaged.

Client: Yeah!!

Now the coach wants to turn the picture of Iron Man into the client. He wants to have the client see himself as that totally unstoppable Iron Man.

Coach: So I want you to see that picture, that posture: leaning forward ready for anything, unstoppable, you can do anything. And this time that picture is you! You're in this picture, ready for anything, unstoppable, totally bad. You're looking determined, thoughtful, your mind fully engaged! Totally bad! Do you see that?

Client: Yeah!! That's what I want!

The more the client is able to feel a particular state, the easier he will find it to build the outcome picture—picture two. The bigger the state is, the more compelling the outcome picture will be.

Notice how the coach is using conversational anchoring by repeating back the client's exact words, including his intonation. The coach will also be using the client's gestures and facial expressions as anchors. The aim is to build up a very powerful state, a state that the client would dearly love to have. The cool part about this is that by building it up, the client gets to experience the state now. This type of anchoring is very important, and it will become even more important when we move on to the conversational versions of the Swish Pattern. We'll talk more about this type of anchoring then.

It's great if your client picks a superhero as their role model. Superheroes have lots of resources—that's what makes them super! Most people will pick somebody more mundane as an archetypal role model, though. They may pick a friend, a family member or a colleague. All these will work fine as long as you identify what it is about the role model that allows them to handle the situation easily, and how this is reflected in their appearance, so that it can be translated into the picture of the new self-image. In addition to overt behavior, the image should reflect the posture, breathing and facial expression of the role model. Remember, the client has to feel the new resources, not just talk about them.

Using this approach to constructing the outcome image has several advantages. It allows the client to engage both their conscious and unconscious minds, and it enables them to construct a rich self-image: one that includes identity, beliefs, values, capabilities and resources, as well as the outward appearances of success and the desired behaviors.

Designing the Swish Pattern using Submodalities

You now have the trigger picture and the outcome picture. Before you run the Swish, you need to determine which submodalities to use in the delivery. This is what we will discuss in this section.

Another Break State

Before you run the Swish, you need to do another break state. You do this because you want the client to feel good after they see the outcome picture. You want the sequence to be:

    1) See trigger picture.

    2) See outcome picture.

    3) Feel fantastic.

This break state simply needs to bring the client down from the peak of their feelings after they have built the outcome picture (rather than before). The good feeling then acts as a reward for the unconscious mind, so that it will continue to show them the outcome picture.

Creating the Swish

In order to do the Swish Pattern, you have to exchange picture one (the trigger picture) and picture two (the outcome picture). You need to do this in such a way that the unconscious mind becomes involved in the process—so that, in the future, it will switch (or "swish") the pictures as soon as the client sees the trigger picture in real life. We're going to talk about several different ways in which you can exchange the two pictures and create the actual Swish. We will start off with the Slingshot Swish Pattern.

The Slingshot Swish Pattern

The Slingshot Swish will work with ninety to ninety-five percent of your clients because it uses the common driving submodalities of size, distance, and brightness. Remember, submodalities are simply the qualities of our internal representations—the pictures that we make in our minds. A visual representation might be in color or black and white. The picture could be a movie picture or a still picture. The picture could be big or small, framed or unframed, two- or three-dimensional. The picture could be a certain size, near or far, to the left or to the right, up or down, fuzzy or clear, bright or dim.

You should be aware that there are some people for whom the Slingshot Swish is not effective because their unconscious mind processes information in an unusual way. You will have to do a little more work with these people to make the Swish truly effective, and we will go through how this is done later on. But first, we will explain the Slingshot Swish Pattern.

When you were young, you may have played with a toy consisting of a ball attached to a bat with a piece of elastic. You would bounce the ball away from the bat, and the elastic would stretch. It would then pull the ball back, and you would be able to hit the ball with the bat again. Imagine you have a picture in front of you that is attached to you with a piece of elastic. You throw the picture away into the distance, but as it moves away the elastic begins to stretch. Finally the elastic becomes so tight that it pulls the picture back toward you. Each time you throw the picture away, the elastic pulls it back. This is the basis of the Slingshot Swish Pattern.

The client sees picture one, the trigger picture, in front of them. They will imagine that the picture is attached to them with a piece of elastic. They will then send picture one off into the distance, far, far away. It needs to be so far away that it becomes a small dot, so that they really cannot make out what the picture is anymore. As the picture moves away and becomes smaller, it will also become darker. The elastic will eventually stretch enough to pull the dot back. However, it pulls it back as the second picture, the outcome picture. The outcome picture will rush toward the client and end up big and bright, right in front of them.

The client will then blank the screen so that no picture is visible. This is essentially a break state for the unconscious mind. The client will then see picture one again, and repeat the process. This conditions the Swish.

Why the Slingshot Swish is So Effective

The Slingshot Swish is very effective because it uses three of the key submodalities: size, distance, and brightness. One or more of these submodalities is likely to be important for the client. A driving submodality is a one that has a major impact on the emotional content of a picture or other internal representation. By "emotional content" we simply mean how the picture makes the client feel.

You can try this out for yourself. Try thinking of a happy memory. Notice what picture comes to mind. Notice where the picture is, how large it is, how bright it is. Notice how the picture makes you feel. Now move the picture further away, and notice how that affects how you feel about it. The chances are that the farther you move the picture away, the less intense your feelings become. Now move the picture back to where it was but make it smaller, and notice how that affects how you feel about it. The chances are that the smaller you make the picture, the less intense your feelings become. Now make the picture the same size as it was but make it dimmer and notice how you feel about it. The chances are that the dimmer you make the picture, the less intense your feelings will become.

Try one final change. This time, make the picture bigger, bring it closer, and make it brighter. Notice how you feel about it now. The chances are that the bigger, closer, and brighter the picture is, the more intense your feelings will be. Now move the picture to wherever feels best, adjust the brightness and size so that you feel comfortable with the level of emotion the picture evokes, and leave it be.

As we have discovered, most people will find that their feelings about an image are directly affected by changes to the size, distance, and brightness of the picture. Using all three of these submodalities in the Slingshot Swish gives you an excellent chance of achieving the result that you want. When you do the Slingshot Swish, the trigger picture will move farther away, and it will get smaller and dimmer. On the return journey, the outcome picture will get closer, bigger, and brighter. Therefore, the client's feelings about picture one should become less intense, and their feelings about picture two should become more intense. This is exactly what you want to happen.

Other Methods of Using the Swish Using Submodalities

Very occasionally you will find that the Slingshot Swish is not effective. This may be because distance, size, and brightness are not major driving submodalities for the client. Alternatively, one—and only one—of those submodalities might be very important, but the client's unconscious mind is confused by the inclusion of the other two. In this case you may need to be more precise in how you perform the Swish.

You can test the effect of changing submodalities, and therefore find a driving submodality, by asking the client to think of a memory of something pleasant and then ask them to:

Move the picture closer and see how they feel. Move the picture farther away and see how they feel. Put the picture back where it was.

Make the picture bigger and see how they feel. Make the picture smaller and see how they feel. Put the picture back as it was.

Make the picture brighter and see how they feel. Make the picture dimmer and see how they feel. Put the picture back as it was.

Turn the picture into a movie and see how they feel. Turn the picture into a still photograph and see how they feel. Put the picture back as it was.

Put a frame around the picture and see how they feel. Take the frame away from the picture and see how they feel. Put the picture back as it was.

Make the picture three-dimensional and see how they feel. Make the picture two-dimensional and see how they feel. Put the picture back as it was.

By going through each of these choices in turn, you can find the submodality or modalities that have the greatest impact on the client. You can then use them to design the Swish.

For example, suppose you find that the size of the picture is a driving submodality, but that distance and brightness are not. In this case you might want to do the Swish entirely on size. You would direct the client to make picture one (the trigger picture) its normal size, and then you would instruct them to embed picture two (the outcome picture) inside picture one very, very small. You would usually ask them to embed the outcome picture either in some detail of picture one (like we did in the example of Janet's cigarette packet), or maybe in the bottom right hand corner if there is nowhere better. You would then run the Swish by having picture two quickly grow in size until it covers picture one.

Delivering the Swish Pattern using Gestures and Voice

The Classical NLP Swish

At this point, you have helped the client to find their trigger picture and their outcome picture, and you have identified the appropriate submodalities. Now you just need to install the Swish—creating a chain leading from the trigger picture to the outcome picture—and then run the Swish enough times to condition the change. You can then test your work.

The Swish Pattern is delivered to the client not just in words, but also using the voice and body of the coach. In this chapter, we will discuss how the coach might deliver the Swish Pattern to the client in the case of a Classic NLP Swish. We will talk about other types of Swish Patterns later on.

In order to get the client's unconscious mind involved, you want to make the process very active and lively.

Before you actually perform the Swish for the client's conscious mind, you perform it purely for her unconscious mind. You set this up by saying, "In a moment, but not yet..." and then describing the steps of the Swish. This allows the client's conscious mind to relax (because it is not being asked to do anything yet). However, the client's unconscious mind will continue to play along with the instructions as you run through the Swish. This allows you to look for the client's unconscious responses, particularly how they respond as the new self-image picture approaches them.

So you may say: "In a moment, but not yet, I am going to ask you to move that picture way into the distance...." Everything you say will be as you say it in the actual Swish, as if the Swish were really being done. The conscious mind relaxes while the unconscious mind goes along with the process.

You might also physically mime taking hold of the client's mental pictures, though you need to know exactly where the pictures are to do this effectively. You might mime moving or throwing picture one out into the distance as you continue to instruct the client verbally in what to do. You may also begin to use a quieter voice as the picture moves away, as if speaking from the location of the picture. Then, you will use the appropriate body language and voice tone as the outcome picture moves back towards the client. You will bring your hand or hands back toward the client, indicating that the picture is returning, while widening them until they reach the final location where you want the outcome picture to be. Your hands will essentially frame the outcome picture. This allows you to make sure that the client is moving and changing the size of the pictures. You can also control the speed at which the pictures move — allowing for a slower Swish at first, while the client gets used to the process, then speeding it up.

You will continue to use your voice to match the movements of your hands and the movement of the picture. So, as the picture moves closer, you can increase the volume of your voice and widen your hands. Similarly, you can change the tone of your voice so that it becomes more excited. This provides valuable nonverbal instruction to the client's unconscious mind.

As the outcome picture moves closer to the client, you will watch for the client's head to move backward slightly. This is the natural physical reaction to something coming close to your face, and it's a valuable calibration tool, particularly if you ask the client to do the Swish by themselves in their own mind. Seeing that head movement lets you know that the client has performed the Swish.

Once you are happy that the client is running the Swish unconsciously, you can also involve the client's conscious mind by saying, "OK, ready? Let's start..." You will then break state by saying, "When I count to three, that picture [trigger picture] will shoot off into the distance. One... Two... Three... Shooting off into the distance... Farther and farther... Getting smaller and smaller..." and so on. Counting to three is not absolutely necessary, but it does allow the client to prepare herself. All this will be accompanied by you using your hands, body, and voice to support the idea of the trigger picture moving off into the distance and the outcome picture returning. Be theatrical! Break state between each repetition by asking the client to "blank the screen." Once you have led the client through the Swish several times, you may ask her to perform the Swish in her own mind a few times. The coach may also ask the client to perform the Swish faster. The visual sense is extremely fast and the faster the Swish runs, the greater the unconscious involvement and the more profound the change.

When you have run the client through the Swish several times, and perhaps asked her to run it in her own mind, it is time to test your work. You will do this by reassociating the client into the context in which she previously experienced the problem and leading her to the point at which she sees the trigger. If the Swish has been effective, then you should see the client unconsciously perform the Swish in her own mind. You will know this is taking place because her head will snap back as the trigger picture moves away and the outcome picture moves closer. You should also see her going into the positive state associated with the outcome. Associate her into several times and places where she had previously experienced the problem to make sure that the change has generalized.

If you find a context where the change has not generalized, then perform the Swish again within that context, as you may have found a different trigger that you have not covered yet.

Combining the Swish Pattern with the New Behavior Generator

The Swish Pattern can be combined with another NLP pattern called the New Behavior Generator. As the name of the pattern suggests, the New Behavior Generator is particularly useful for extending the Swish into the area of generative change. While the Classical Swish may primarily cause a change in a specific behavior, the New Behavior Generator is designed to offer an embodied experience of possibilities.

Some trainers run courses where the high point of the course is an experience such as the fire walk. In the fire walk, you'll actually walk across a bed of hot coals. Although it is quite possible for the human foot to withstand the heat of these coals as long as a normal walking speed is maintained, it seems impossible, and that's the key. The fire walk forces you to realize that the boundaries you have set for yourself can be breached, and you can extend your range of possibilities. Although the New Behavior Generator does not have the glamour of a fire walk, it is designed with the same goal.

In the New Behavior Generator, you associate into somebody who you believe has more possibilities than yourself. When combined with the Swish, the New Behavior Generator allows the client to step into her future, ideal self and experience what it is like to be that person of unlimited potential. Once she has had this experience, she will never be able to go back to who she was!

Combining the two patterns can be really fun, and it's something that you as the coach will also enjoy. Your client actually gets to step into their new identity at the end of the Swish Pattern. This will make them feel awesome, and you'll get to see their reaction. Practicing with the Swish and New Behavior Generator allows you to see the power of your work. During your next practice session, try this pattern out and see the result. Make sure that the outcome picture, the new self-identity, is so compelling to the client—so amazing, so awesome, so limitless in possibility—that the client has an incredible experience stepping into the picture. Like the fire walk, it will act as a ritual that allows them to take on their new identity and then take it home with them in a very real way. Before we describe how to combine the two patterns, we will briefly outline how the New Behavior Generator works.

The New Behavior Generator

The New Behavior Generator is an NLP pattern designed to install a new behavior in a certain context. In NLP our clients typically have four types of problems:

> 1) They don't feel something that they want to feel, such as motivation.
>
> 2) They feel something that they don't want to feel, such as fear.
>
> 3) They do something that they don't want to do, such as a bad habit.
>
> 4) They don't do something that they want to do, such as finishing their great novel.

With the last category, it could be that they simply do not have the motivation to do what they want to do, so this is really the result of the first category of problems. The client doesn't feel a sense of motivation and therefore she does not do what she is not motivated to do. On the other hand, it could simply be that the client does not have a memory or other reference experience of the behavior that they want to do. They have never done the behavior, they've never been able to do the behavior, and there is simply no part of their neurology that is set up to do the behavior. In this case, they need to build a new part that will be responsible for the new behavior.

The way a person would traditionally install a new behavior is by going to a vocational school to learn how to "do" the behavior. I have no part of myself that cuts hair so I go to hairdressing college and it builds a part of me that cuts hair. Simple. While we are not suggesting that NLP can teach you how to cut hair, we are saying that NLP can be very efficient at installing the part that will be responsible for some new behavior. Supposing you want a part of you that will approach and speak to people in bars. This doesn't require you to go to school; it simply requires that you have a part of yourself that is responsible for the behavior. The New Behavior Generator would be a suitable pattern for this.

Steps of the New Behavior Generator:

> 1) Identify the outcome for the new behavior. This outcome needs to be what is called, in NLP terms, "well formed." This means that it is specific, positively stated (what the client wants, not what he doesn't want), contextual (he must know the context in which he wants the new behavior to appear) and sensory-based (he knows what he will see, hear and feel when he has the outcome). The outcome should also be ecological and worthwhile. An ecological outcome is essentially one that is good for all of you, in all aspects of your life. For

example, if I were to say I want to work hard all the time, this would not be ecological because I would not have time to spend with my family (or to eat and sleep, for that matter)!

2) Identify a reference experience for the behavior that will lead to the desired outcome. As in the description of the Swish, this reference experience could be something from the client's own experience, or it could be the experience of an archetype who is able to embody the behavior and get the outcome. The archetype could be drawn from a character in a movie or a book. It could be a historical figure, or somebody the client knows from his own life. He could even imagine doing the new behavior himself as long as he imagines it in a compelling enough way.

3) Identify a "movie," a sequence of images, which shows the behavior being carried out and the outcome being achieved. This could be a movie from the client's memory of himself. Alternatively, it could be a movie from his imagination, showing the archetype performing the behavior and achieving the outcome. This movie should be dissociated, meaning that the client should see himself in it as if watching the movie from a seat in a movie theater. Make sure the movie is just the way the client would want it to look, with him or the archetype performing the new behavior perfectly.

4) Associate your client into the movie by inviting him to step or float into the "him" on the screen, so he can see feel what it feels like from the inside. Make sure it is perfect from an associated position, and make any appropriate editorial changes. It may be necessary to dissociate the client from the movie

to make these changes by asking him to step or float back to the "seat in the theater." Once the client has made any necessary changes, associate him into the movie again to make sure it is perfect from the inside.

5) Make sure the client is truly happy with the new behavior, while watching and listening for any unconscious objections. For example, if you ask the client if he would be happy with the new behavior and he says "yes" in a doubtful tone of voice, then you should ask him about any doubts he has. Assuming he is entirely happy with the experience, suggest that he absorb it unconsciously: "You can begin to absorb this on a deep unconscious level…"

6) Future pace and test the new part by having the client imagine the next time he might need this behavior. Once again, pay particular attention to any sign of doubt in his voice or manner. For example, if he says, "Yes…I guess that's good…" then you have missed some aspect of the change. Ask him, "What was that?" or, "What's happening now?" to discover the source of the doubt. Once any problems have been addressed, you can run the New Behavior Generator one last time to make sure it is fully installed.

The Difference Between the New Behavior Generator and the Swish Pattern

The New Behavior Generator and the Swish are very different patterns. The Swish uses a client's existing desire to move toward a new identity, or to install a new identity in a specific context. The intention is to create generative change. In contrast, the New Behavior Generator creates a new behavior for the client that will be triggered in a certain context. So on the surface, the Swish creates a new identity, while the New Behavior Generator creates a part responsible for a specific behavior.

But we know from our discussion of the history of the Swish that it can be used to change a behavior while also creating generative change at the identity level. This is true because all experience is multilevel. At any moment in time we are not simply existing, not simply doing something in a behavioral way; we are also feeling a particular way, believing, valuing, and holding a sense of our own self-identity. So behavior begets identity, and identity begets behavior. They are intertwined and cannot be separated. Combining the Swish with the New Behavior Generator installs a new identity level that can create generative change, while also installing a new part for a new behavior aimed at achieving a specific new outcome. It combines new identity with new behavior and everything in between such as beliefs, values, and emotional resources.

The NBG Swish

For the sake of brevity we will call the combined pattern the NBG Swish. It requires some minor modifications from the Swish Pattern you have already learned. The main difference is that the process ends not with an outcome picture, but with an outcome movie — a movie that has all the qualities and power of the client's desired outcome. This will result in a much richer representation of the outcome while also being more specific as regards behavior. In fact, the outcome image has to be a movie because it involves a behavior. The client needs to see and then experience himself performing the new behavior. The first frame of the movie will be a picture of the client's new self, the middle frame (or frames) will be that new self engaging in the new behavior, and the final frame will be their new self achieving the desired outcome.

The client will have designed and directed the movie under your guidance, using the New Behavior Generator as outlined above. During this process the client will have watched the outcome movie from both a dissociated position (watching it on a movie screen) and an associated position (from inside the movie). This should make it very easy for the client to reassociate into the outcome movie in the steps to follow.

Let's work this through with an example. George is a writer with writer's block. Each time he sits down to write he sees the blank screen on his computer and his notebooks full of notes and he freezes. Inside his mind he is making pictures of himself writing stories, none of which meet his high standards. So then he makes movies of himself editing the stories and creating new stories that also fail to meet his standards; he feels overwhelmed by the material that he has accumulated and yet is unable to turn it into words on the screen.

Running the NBG Swish, we first help George to develop a new self-image that will replace the image he currently holds of himself as being unable to write stories worth reading. When we ask George how he will be as a person when writer's block is no longer an issue for him, he slowly begins to craft an image of a man who is experiencing the world in a new and unique way. This man is intensely curious and adventurous and his primary motivation is to experience. The writing comes second, and he writes because he has something worth saying. This new self-image becomes the opening frame of the New Behavior Generator movie.

From this we move to his desired outcome, which has changed from wishing to write a book to wanting to share his experiences of the world. This widens the outcome so that it is no longer about the book; the book is still in the outcome, but this time he sees himself at a book signing, sharing his stories on a personal basis with the audience. The book is secondary. This becomes the final scene of the New Behavior Generator movie.

All we have to do now is to link the opening frame with the final scene. What happens in the movie to get from the identity that he has to the outcome that he wants? What behaviors does he have to engage in? It is not appropriate or even possible to build the movie frame by frame, at least not on the cognitive basis, because too much time will lapse in the "real" movie—George's life—in the several months leading up to the book signing. We may have George run through the entire experience in a formal "eyes-closed" trance later on, but for now we will just build two or three scenes to represent the behaviors that George will have to engage in to reach his outcome scene. George chooses three scenes to create. In the first, he is planning a trip to a small town that will be used as a location in the book. In the second scene he is visiting this town, exploring and speaking to the people there, asking them for their stories. In the third scene he is sharing his experiences with his writing club friends while recording the conversation for later transcription.

We now have a short movie. The actor in the movie is the new George: a man who experiences the world in a new and unique way and then shares his story. This new George begins to prepare for his trip to the town, and the scene shifts to him actually visiting the town. The scene shifts again to the new George sharing his experiences with his friends, and finally it moves to the book reading and signing as the final scene.

You'll notice that there is no scene in the movie of George actually writing. George seemed very congruent with the movie as it was, so we expected that the writing would take care of itself once the new identity was installed, which proved to be the case.

Doing the NBG Swish

You will now run the NBG Swish in the usual way, with the trigger picture being the trigger for the problem, and the outcome picture being the first frame of the outcome movie. You will lead the client to embed the first frame of the outcome movie within the trigger picture. You will then do the Swish using the slingshot technique, or some other version of the Swish using driving submodalities. You will blank the screen and repeat as before until it has been installed in the client and then you can test by asking the client to think of the trigger picture and watching his reaction. Typically his head will move backwards as the unconscious mind presents him with the first frame of the outcome movie.

In the case of George the writer, the image of the new George (which he saw as an emoticon of a smiling face) was embedded in the power switch of his computer. We conditioned the Swish by running it several times. Now each time he turns on his computer, or wakes it up from hibernation, the smiling face expands and turns into the picture of the new George.

It may be a good idea to do the above pattern with the client standing up, so they can step into the opening frame of the New Behavior Generator movie in the step that follows. However, if preferred, the client can be sitting down, or even in a formal trance, and they can step into the movie in their imagination.

Stepping into the Outcome Picture

Finally, you will invite the client to step into the outcome picture so you can invite them to experience the outcome movie from an associated position (from inside the movie). You will invite them to run the movie to the end until they have the desired outcome. To guide them through that journey, you might say something like this: "I would like you to step into that new you that you see in front of you. Feel how good it feels as you do that. And as you step into that new you, feel yourself in that movie—see what you are seeing; hear what you are hearing; feel what you are feeling. Feel what it feels like to engage in those new behaviors, knowing that you are moving toward your outcome. Notice what is happening as you do that, and how the people around you are reacting. Feel yourself moving through the whole movie, until you achieve the outcome at the end."

In the case of our writer, George, once we had conditioned the Swish Pattern so that each time he saw the power switch on his computer the smiling face would expand into the new George, we took him into a deep trance. Then we ran the NBG Swish while he was in trance. We suggested to George that he visualize the power switch on his computer. We were immediately able to see George's reaction as the Swish was unconsciously triggered. We ran the Swish once more and this time suggested that he step into the new George. We noticed a wonderful physiological shift as he did so. We then allowed him to fully experience the movie from beginning to end from this associated position.

Using the NBG Swish in Practice

The NBG Swish is a useful and entertaining pattern that your clients will love. The pattern can take some time because it has so many moving parts to design, build, and run. The NBG Swish is a great way to unconsciously install a new behavior because the Swish portion of the pattern can be repeated several times very quickly, and it can be very efficiently linked to the trigger. This means that the new behavior can be installed in a very specific context.

The Swish Pattern as a Recovery Strategy

In this chapter we will describe how the Swish can be used as a Recovery Strategy. A Recovery Strategy seeks to answer the question, "What should the client do if things go wrong?"

The Swish is a wonderfully powerful pattern for changing behavior. As a result of it, your clients will find themselves not only changing their specific problem behavior but also making other generative changes in their lives. However, nothing works all of the time, for all people, in all situations. There will be times when you have led the client through a wonderful Swish Pattern, have seen real change occur in your office, have future paced the new behaviors, and have done everything else humanly possible to ensure that the change was successful. And yet the client goes out and engages in the same problem behavior. An example of how this can occur in practice is with smokers. Someone who visits your office as a smoker may leave totally free of the power of cigarettes. They may go for weeks, months, or even years without smoking. And then, one day, perhaps they go out with their friends and they have some drinks, and one of their friends challenges them to go outside and smoke a cigarette. Because they have had some drinks, their willpower is a little less than usual, so they agree to the challenge. Suddenly they are a "smoker" again. They disregard the fact that they have only smoked one cigarette and that they hadn't smoked for six months. Instead, they focus on the fact that they have smoked, which they take to mean that they are a smoker. In NLP we call this kind of thought—"I smoked a cigarette so I'm a smoker again"—black-and-white thinking. It's all or nothing.

In this section we will discuss the use of Recovery Strategies to deal with those times when your client falls off the wagon in spite of the change work that you did with them. A Recovery Strategy is simply a set of links that we attach onto the end of a behavioral chain to lead in a new direction. Think of it this way: when we do the Classical Swish we are building a chain that begins with the trigger picture. The trigger picture used to lead to unwanted behavior, but with the new chain created by the Swish, it now leads in a new direction. The Recovery Strategy takes a slightly different approach: it follows the original chain but adds new links onto the end so that it ends in a new place.

You know how, in a scary movie, the teenager always decides to go through the front door of the haunted house on Halloween? Nobody in their right mind would actually go through that door, just as nobody in their right mind would smoke a cigarette after they'd quit. Yet they do! The Classical Swish Pattern is like having the teenager's mother waiting by the front door of the haunted house with her arms crossed saying, "Don't go inside!" Similarly, your client might want to smoke another cigarette, but the Swish Pattern puts their new self-image on guard against that. In spite of everything, the teenager goes into the haunted house, just as your client decides to smoke a cigarette on a Friday night after a few drinks with her friends. A Recovery Strategy is like leaving the back door of the haunted house open. Even though the teenager goes through the front door, she can escape through the back door. For your smoking client, the Recovery Strategy can allow her to feel like even more of a successful non-smoker after she smokes that one cigarette.

A simple example of a Recovery Strategy is to tell the recovered smoker that: "You will not know that you are a non-smoker until you have smoked at least one more cigarette and found that they no longer have a hold over you. In fact, from this point on, each time you smoke a cigarette, you will find it more repulsive and sickening; you will be more confident that you are taking the right path for your health; and you will be more certain of your ability to be the person that you want to be, smoke-free." This type of double-blind allows a smoker to use the fact that he just smoked as proof that he is a non-smoker. And the more times he smokes, the more proof he has that he is a non-smoker. You are chaining another representation (in this case using words) onto the end of the problem behavior, so your client can recover if they happen to fall off the wagon.

In the case of a smoker, they have smoked a cigarette and there's nothing we can do about that fact. If we did not give them the recovery strategy, they might run a chain of the following representations: cigarette they smoked in the bar > image of themselves as a smoker > begin smoking again. They have essentially done a "problem Swish" on themselves and installed a new self-image of themselves as a smoker! We need to install a new Swish: cigarette they smoked in the bar > image of themselves as a non-smoker > continue their healthy habits. In order to do this we must chain the pictures together, but if we simply tell them (with words) that the next cigarette they smoke will mean that they are a non-smoker, the picture of them as a non-smoker may not appear in the chain. Instead, if we install the chain using images, there is more chance that the positive chain will be there if they need it.

Since we already know how to do the Swish, it is very easy to install the recovery strategy using it. We will use the smoker as an easy example, but of course it can be generalized to any other problem behavior.

Here is the pattern:

1) Find a context where the client may fall off the wagon and return to the old problem behavior. With a smoker, it might be when they go out with their friends to a bar, or with a particular group of friends who always smoke, or perhaps at work if they have a particularly stressful day. Find out where they might be when they would be most likely to smoke again, or to engage in the problem behavior. If you know where they smoke most of their cigarettes now, you already have a short list of the places where they are most likely to fall off the wagon. Since the Swish is a very quick pattern to perform and benefits from repetition, you can install the recovery strategy in each of these locations.

2) Find out what they would be likely to see that would let them know that they were engaging in the problem behavior again. So, in the case of the smoker, it could be seeing a cigarette in their hand — or even seeing another person smoking, which could mean they are hanging around outside with other smokers (at least in New York, where smoking is banned in all public buildings). This will be the trigger picture.

3) Find out what they would see that would let them know that this is not part of their identity, it was simply something that they did which is over (even though they have fallen off the wagon this once). This picture may be more difficult to find, particularly if they are a black-and-white thinker. You may want to use a metaphor, for example, of a client who quit, smoked one more time and realized how terrible it made her feel. Your client could decide to create a picture of themselves as somebody like that: the sort of person who smokes a cigarette and discovers that not only does that not make you a smoker, in fact it makes you someone who is even more of a non-smoker.

4) Now you run the Swish. The client has two pictures: one being what they will see when they have fallen off the wagon, and one of themselves as somebody whose identity is not determined by what they did in the past—someone determined to be the person they want to be in the future.

Take the first picture—perhaps a picture of a hand with a cigarette—and embed the second picture, the client-as-they-want-to-be picture. Do the Swish so that the first picture moves into the distance on the slingshot, and the client-as-they-want-to-be picture comes back to replace it. Blank the screen and repeat. Blank the screen and repeat. (Don't forget that the structure of the Swish should be based upon the driving submodalities of the client.)

5) Now future pace. Get them to think of a time in the future when they might fall off the wagon. Have them imagine falling off the wagon, and notice what happens. Ask them what meaning they attach to that event. Does it make them a smoker again, or is it just something that happened which does not affect the fact that they are a non-smoker?

The danger with this technique is that the client could imagine themselves smoking in the future and think that that is no big deal. This could encourage them to go back to their old behavior once in a while. For this reason you might also want to attach a suggestion that each cigarette they smoke in the future will taste worse than the one before. The more they smoke, the worse the cigarettes will taste. If you are installing this type of posthypnotic suggestion, of course, you'll want to use your voice and your face to convey the nasty taste to the client's unconscious mind. When you are discussing the first cigarette, you will have a slight look of distaste on your face; by the third cigarette you will look and sound thoroughly disgusted, and by the fifth you will be practically vomiting.

If you are doing a first smoking session with a client, you may wish to use the simple verbal recovery strategy described at the start of the chapter, telling your **Client:** "You will not know that you are a healthy non-smoker until you have smoked again and realized that cigarettes no longer have power over you. In fact, the more cigarettes you smoke, the more you will realize this and you may have to smoke another three or even four cigarettes to be totally certain you are free of them." If, on the other hand, you have a smoking client who returns and reports that she has gone back to smoking after a period of being smoke-free, you may wish to spend more time and do the full Swish Recovery Strategy.

The Hypnotic Swish Pattern

This book is designed to allow the Swish to be used in a number of contexts, including by classical hypnotists, and in this chapter we will discuss how to use the Swish during hypnosis and deep trance.

Once you understand how to use the Swish during your hypnotic trance work, it will become a very potent tool for you. In fact, if you wanted to, you could use the Swish Pattern with virtually all your clients, and on virtually any issue. It is truly that versatile. In order to give you maximum flexibility, we will present three variations of the Hypnotic Swish. In the first variation we will assume that you have performed a Classical Swish (as described in earlier chapters) when your client is in a more uptime state, and that you wish to repeat the Swish Pattern when your client is in trance to deepen the effects. In the second variation we will show you how to do a Swish while the client is in a normal waking state, and use the Swish itself as a trance induction, so that it is seamlessly integrated into the trance process. In the third variation we will do the Swish entirely in trance, relying on unconscious processing and the unconscious mind's ability to implement the Swish.

Variation One: Repeating the Swish Pattern in the Trance State

In this variation of the Hypnotic Swish, you will do the Classical Swish Pattern with the client at the start of the session, while they are in a normal state of awareness. You can use any of the variations of the Swish described earlier in the book. You will then put your client into trance and simply repeat the same pattern, this time when they are in trance. The variation that we describe here uses auditory anchors. Remember that we include visual anchors in the Classical Swish by moving our hands away from the client and then back toward them. But during hypnosis the client's eyes are probably closed, so in this variation the client will hear the coach making sounds and those sounds become anchored into the process. Here is the sequence for the first variation:

1) Find the context and the trigger picture, as in the Classical Swish.

2) When you find the outcome picture, you will add one additional step: ask the client what the sound of the outcome picture would be if it were a sound? This sounds like a very strange question, but it has two important functions within the hypnotic version of the Swish: firstly, this sound will become an auditory anchor for the outcome state. The benefit of an auditory anchor is that it can be used easily and rapidly when the client is in a closed-eye trance. Secondly, sounds activate a very primitive and powerful area of the brain.

Sounds, especially the sounds that we can make with our own bodies (shouts, screams, cries, laughter), have been with us far longer than language has. Human language is a relatively new development in the history of mankind, one which went hand-in-hand with the development of the brain's prefrontal cortex and what we think of as our rational and logical mind, the mind that speaks to us inside our own head.

Because our rational brain has essentially hijacked the sound-creating part of the brain, we now get a little embarrassed by making sounds in a public context because, by doing so, we are sharing our deepest emotional state with the strangers around us. For example, we may make a sound of appreciation, or joy, and then feel a moment of embarrassment when we look around to see who noticed it. This may sound like a minor point, but it is not. Think back to the Democratic primaries for the 2008 presidential election. One of the candidates is Howard Dean, the former governor of Vermont. Howard Dean is giving a rousing speech, firing up his supporters. His supporters are cheering loudly, and the governor joins in. At first he shouts out the names of the states that he will be visiting on the campaign trail, but then he simply screams into the microphone. Not a word but a primeval sound, something like "yyyeeeeaaahhhh!!!" Of course, because the governor was miked, that scream sounded ridiculously loud compared to the background noise. It is said that it was the repeated playing of that scream on the nightly news shows that destroyed Dean's chances of being president. If Howard Dean's shout didn't echo around the world, it certainly echoed around the Democratic presidential campaign race!

By asking the client to make a sound associated with the outcome, we are asking the client to "do a Howard Dean." We are asking them to get back in touch with their own emotional and primeval sound, which allows the sound portion of their brain to go back to what it was originally designed for: making sound. And because we are asking the client to use the sound portion of their brain to make sound, it becomes temporarily unavailable for thinking in words. So this request provides the unconscious mind the opportunity to step forward while the conscious mind takes a short break.

When the client presents us with the sound, it should have the "feel" of the identity that the client would like. Because we're not used to making sounds, the client is likely to offer us a very weak and unappealing sound at first. If they do so, you should not accept it. Rather, you should repeat it back to them with some amplification and continue doing so until a suitably rousing primeval shout or scream is produced.

Client: Ah.

Coach: You mean E-ah?

Client: A-ah!

Coach: Oh, you mean A-Hah!

Client: A-ha!

Coach: A-HAAAH!

Client: A-HAAAH!

If you are uncomfortable with this process—perhaps your client is an elderly lady—you can simply choose to click your fingers to anchor the Swish. If you do decide to use the finger click, then make sure you use it while you are doing the Swish in the waking state so that it will become anchored when you do it in trance. Also, do not click your fingers too close to the client's ear, as it can bring them out of trance.

Once you have obtained the sound, it acts as an auditory anchor for the outcome state. When the client is in trance, you will use their sound to fire off the Swish and replace the trigger picture with the outcome picture. This is simple to do. Suppose the client wants to be confident when they are with a customer. The trigger picture is the face of a customer who looks a little "defensive." The client creates an outcome picture of himself or herself looking totally confident, completely in control, and very calm. When asked to choose a sound reflecting the state, they choose this: "Bu-AAH!" When you do the Swish Pattern, before the formal trance begins, ask the client to see the face of the customer and then embed the outcome picture of himself or herself right in the center of the customer's forehead. You will then get them to perform the Swish so that the calm, confident picture of themselves flows out of the center of their customer's forehead and into the space in between them and the customer. You will say something like this: "I want you to see your customer there in front of you, and right in the middle of their forehead you see that picture of yourself. Now when I make the sound 'Bu-AAH' I want that picture of yourself to come out of their forehead and to appear in the space in between you and them. Ready?... One... two... three... 'Bu-AAH.'"

So "Bu-AAH" becomes the signal for the Swish. Because they are now used to the sound "Bu-AAH," meaning "do the Swish," they automatically do it when they hear the sound again later on in trance.

During the trance, when you wish to do the Swish, you simply say something like: "So now when you see the face of the customer...Bu-AAH... and every time you see the face of the customer...Bu-AAH." And so on. Of course, you will still be calibrating to make sure that they are doing the Swish.

An Example of a Hypnotic Swish

The following example is taken from a client session. The hypnotist has done the Swish with the client using the slingshot method. The hypnotist has used a finger click to indicate the movement of the trigger picture into the distance, and used the word "two" to indicate the outcome picture moving back towards the client. So the Swish was anchored to the sounds, bracketed here to indicate their auditory nature: [click] and [two].

Toward the end of the session, the client had gone into trance spontaneously, and the hypnotist had reinforced the work done earlier in the session by using the instruction [click] [two] to run the Swish Pattern. Whilst running the Swish Pattern in the trance, the hypnotist was calibrating the unconscious response of the subject. The client would relax slightly to the finger snap, then the client's head would move back on [two]. When the coach was saying "that's right" and "thank you," she was ratifying to the client's unconscious mind that the client was doing the Swish correctly.

A standard end-of-trance protocol is included at the end of the trance, including instructions for selective amnesia, general ego building, deeper induction and trance ratification.

Most of what was said as part of this example simply reflected explanations that have been given to the client in a waking state prior to the unconscious Swish. Therefore, the actual words used in this trance should not be taken as a script that could be used with other clients. But hopefully this will give you some ideas as to how the Swish can be incorporated into a trance once it has been set up in the more conscious portion of a session. Here is the trance script:

"So when you go into trance, then you can start to see one of those times, one of those contexts, where you previously had that problem. You can see that picture in front of you, that's right, thank you, and [click] off into the distance, [two], thank you, and now you can see another context where you used to have the problem and it can [click] and shoot off into the distance, [two], that's right, and now you can pick another context and it can [click] [two], very good! And now because the unconscious mind is basically a machine for generalizing it can begin to do this process [click] [two] inside [click] [two]… it's all ready [click] [two] to do so and the great thing about the unconscious mind [click] [two] is that it's able to do things very, very fast [click] [two] [click] [two] [click] [two] so you can get a lot of generalization inside, [click] [two] [click] [two] very good, that's right, continue to make all those changes, [click] [two] [click] [two] because the faster the unconscious mind processes the deeper and more profound the changes [click] [two] [click] [two] and this pattern can fire up automatically so as soon as you see that first picture [click] [two] the second one automatically comes up [click] [two]... the person that you want to be, the person that you're already becoming, each and every time [click] you're in this context, [two] right [click] [two].

"And before you come back into the room on a count of three I want to say that you can consciously remember everything that will be beneficial for you to remember and as for the rest you can simply find that it's easy to forget, and you can forget this process [click] [two] until you're in the situation, the context, [click] [two] when it will be beneficial for your unconscious to [click] [two] remind you of the person that you're already becoming [click] [two]. Because you are a wonderful person...[click] [two] and a wonderful hypnotic subject [click] [two]... and the next time you go into trance you can go even deeper and so now I'm going to count to three and when I reach three you'll find yourself back in the room feeling awake alert and absolutely fantastic. One... aware of your body in the chair...[click] [two] ... your eyes beginning to flutter... three... coming fully and completely back in the room feeling awake alert and fantastic! WOW – great job!"

Variation Two: The Swish as a Trance Induction

In this variation of the Hypnotic Swish, you will actually use the Swish as a trance induction, or to deepen the trance. You will start off, prior to the trance, by asking the client what they want to work through, obtaining the context in which they want to change, and finding the trigger picture. You will then begin the trance. You could do a formal trance induction followed by the process described below, which will then act as a deepener. Alternatively, you could simply ask the client to close their eyes and then use the process described below (which, as you will see, is similar to the NBG Swish) to begin the trance, as an induction. You will have your client with their eyes closed, either in trance or about to go into trance. Now you're going to instruct the client to go through the following process to create the outcome picture:

> 1) Imagine relaxing in a comfortable seat in a movie theater. This imaginary movie theater will allow you to create a picture of your outcome, and it will be fun!

> 2) As you continue to relax in that chair, you can see a movie on the screen of somebody dealing with the same situation, which they want to change, and dealing with it in a totally resourceful way. If you wish, you can see somebody on the screen that you admire, and who you know could deal easily with the situation.

> 3) You are the director of the movie and can make any changes that are needed. At the end of this process the person on screen should be handling the situation perfectly. Being the director gives you control over the resources, the feelings, the beliefs, and the values of the person on screen.

> 4) As you relax comfortably, you slowly begin to realize that the person on the screen is you.

> 5) Float into the screen and experience the movie from the inside, from inside that person on the screen. See what they see, hear what they hear, and feel what they feel!

6) Float back to the chair in the movie theater and make any necessary changes so that the movie is perfect from both outside and inside. When you have a complete and perfect movie, float back into it and try it on again, seeing what you see, hearing what you hear, and feeling what you feel.

7) Float back out to the theater. Now shrink the picture down until it is small.

By asking the client to imagine being in the movie theater, seeing themselves on the screen, and then to float into themselves and experience things from the inside, we are asking them to create positive hallucinations with visual, auditory and kinesthetic elements. Having positive hallucinations is a trance phenomenon and this experience will induce or deepen trance naturally.

You will now lead the client through the Swish itself. Let's go back to our example of the client who wants to be more confident in front of his customers. You would ask him to: "See the face of the customer, this time with the picture of the ideal you embedded in the customer's forehead, as if someone has stuck a stamp on it. When I click my fingers, that picture will Swish out of your customer's forehead, grow to life-size and appear in the space between you and him. When it does, step forward into that new you, ready to greet your customer...One two three CLICK..." The hypnotist may once again want to have the client generate a sound that will symbolize that outcome state. This sound can be used to set off the Swish as in variation one.

Variation Three: Relying on Unconscious Processing

Unconscious processing relies upon the ability of the mind to restructure itself in a beneficial way outside of conscious awareness. There may be times when you as a hypnotist may wish to rely on the client's unconscious mind, rather than on a more formal and cognitive process like the Swish. Examples of times when you may wish to use this approach include:

1) As a closing technique at the end of the session. This gives you the opportunity to instruct the client's unconscious mind to make any changes required to integrate their new learning, or deal with any part of the issue that may have been missed in the session. This type of "process instruction" need only take a minute or two and can be included in a piece of trance work prior to bringing the client out of trance. In fact, we would encourage you to have a standard piece of process instruction that you can include in all of your sessions.

2) When the client herself is not aware of the details of her issue. This happens when the unconscious mind has decided to protect the person by keeping details of the issue outside of their conscious awareness. Using process instruction allows the unconscious mind to deal with the issue while still maintaining its secrecy.

3) As a powerful technique in its own right when dealing with a deep trance subject. For many clients, trance results in an almost complete lack of conscious awareness. Very deep and profound work can be done with the unconscious mind in the absence of conscious interference.

If you wish, you may even rely entirely on unconscious processing to locate the synesthesia and resources that the client needs. You could use the outline script below as the basis of a Hypnotic Swish Pattern using purely unconscious processing. It could be inserted into any hypnotic trance. It is based on a session with a smoker who reported feeling stress in the office with his boss, but it can easily be adapted to other issues. The script assumes that the hypnotist is familiar with catalepsy, which, in the world of hypnosis, is when a client moves or holds a part of their body without conscious awareness. We all experience catalepsy everyday— for example, when we hold a drink in our hand during a conversation in a bar or restaurant and "forget" we are holding it. In change work, however, catalepsy often takes the form of the client's arm or hand "floating" or rising through in the air following a suggestion from the hypnotist. If you have not worked with catalepsy before as a coach, you can simply give more general instruction without reference to the "rising arm" included in the example below. Here's the hypnotic script:

"… and as you begin to drift deeper into trance I would like you to consider that you came here today for a very important reason; you came here today to make an important change in your life. And your unconscious has begun to consider how you will be as a person when you have made this change in your life and become a healthy non-smoker. I would like your unconscious now to create an image in your mind, an image of how you will be when you have made this change.

"And it's not important whether or not your unconscious mind chooses to share this image with your conscious mind, or whether your unconscious chooses to keep this image in the background. What is important is that your unconscious begins to understand how you'll be as a person now that you've made this change, how you will be as a person when you are already a healthy non-smoker, now, with all the resources that you need to deal with those times in your life when you wish to feel relaxed.

"And as your unconscious creates that image, I would like this arm [hypnotist lifts the client's left arm] to begin rising only as quickly as you can find all the resources that you will have when you've made this change. I don't know what those resources will be, when you are able to take care of yourself and keep yourself healthy, and when you are able to remain calm in all those situations when you would like to feel calm. That's right. [Left arm continues to rise.]

"And as your unconscious creates this image, you begin to notice how you're different in this picture when you have all those resources that you need, just as you're beginning to realize that what's really important to you is feeling healthy inside, where changes are already beginning to take place. As you look at that picture you will begin to see that other changes, taking place on the inside, can also be seen on the outside. That could be the glow of your healthy skin, your clear eyes, the way you can breathe easily and deeply, and an overall sense of confidence that comes from knowing that you're in control.

"Thank you. Now I would like you to make that picture bigger, make it brighter, and move it a little closer. That way you can really enjoy looking at that picture, knowing that this is the person whom you are already becoming. You have already stepped out on the path to becoming this person and all you have to do is to keep moving.

"In a moment, but not yet, I would like you to go back to that time in the office that we talked about. Only this time it will be different. This time as soon as your boss steps into your office, I would like your unconscious to show you this picture that you just made of yourself, the healthy non-smoker, confident and breathing deeply. And to make it easy, I will lead you through the experience: you are in the office, your boss walks in, and you see that picture of yourself as a healthy non-smoker, confident and breathing deeply. And as you see that picture you feel that sense of calmness, confidence, and relaxation. Now blank the screen. You are in the office, your boss steps in, and you see that picture of yourself in control, a healthy non-smoker, seeing that confidence and breathing deeply, and as you see that picture you feel that sense of calmness, confidence, and relaxation.

"And now I would like your unconscious mind to begin to search through your memories, and to find all those times when you saw your boss's face, and each time you do that the picture of the new you appears in front of you, and you feel calm, confident, and relaxed. And I don't want this arm [touching left arm] to begin sinking down to your lap any faster than you can go through each and every one of those memories, and have this new image appear in front of you, and those new feelings of calmness, confidence, and relaxation grow inside.

"That's right. Each time you see your boss's face, that new picture appears, and as you see the new picture you feel calm, confident, and relaxed."

Now that you have mastered the Hypnotic Swish, you will find that it's a powerful technique to keep in your hypnotic toolbox. Feel free to use it liberally with your clients and you will have great results.

The Conversational Swish Pattern

The Swish Pattern can also be delivered conversationally, which means it can be used in business coaching—when the Classical Swish might not be appropriate. The version of the Conversational Swish described here is based upon John Overdurf's wonderful coaching pattern.

There have been a number of business coaches who have attended our NLP training courses in New York. Although they are often impressed and amazed with the NLP techniques they learn, they are concerned about how they will use the techniques in their own practice. They may be coaching very senior executives and they don't want to do techniques that are "unusual," such as patterns requiring their clients to make pictures in their minds and move those pictures around—patterns like the Swish! They are afraid that their clients will think that they are strange or crazy, which could jeopardize their jobs. However, if you are a business coach you may want to have a Swish Pattern available, so it's good to know that the Swish can be done in a purely conversational way.

The Conversational Swish allows you to install a new chain of representations and a new behavior in your client without them being aware of exactly what you are doing or how you are doing it. They will simply feel a different way about things and find their behavior changing. In fact, by using the Conversational Swish, they might find that their entire life is transformed without knowing how!

If you do most or all of your coaching over the telephone, then you need to be able to lead your client through the Swish Pattern without being there in front of them or being able to use your hands to show them where to move the pictures. The pattern described in this chapter overcomes that difficulty so that your telephone coaching with the Swish is seamless and transformative.

The steps of the Swish will be the same as those discussed for the Classical Swish in Chapter Four. However, the method for obtaining each of the pictures, and the method for running the Swish itself, will be a little different. As you read the description of the steps, remember that your objective is to get the client to see what they see before they have the problem (the trigger), create a dissociated picture of how they want to be instead (the outcome), find a method to perform the Swish, and then condition it through repetition.

Here are the steps.

1) Find the context. It is necessary, even in business coaching, to find the context; if you don't, then the resource will not be attached to the correct external stimulus. What this means is that your subject will not feel the way they want to feel, will not be the person they want to be, and will not behave the way they want to behave at the actual time that they need to. The context acts as an anchor for the resource, and to find it you simply need to ask them the usual question: "When was the last time this happened?" You can then transition into the present tense: "Where are you when this is happening?" And, of course, you want to get sensory information: "What are you seeing that lets you know that?" When in the middle of a conversation, none of these questions seem out of the ordinary. However, it is really important that you track your client's responses and backtrack as necessary to find any information that you may have missed, and to check that you have actually found the right context and the right trigger.

2) Find the trigger image, the visual portion of the synesthesia. Remember, the synesthesia is the combination of the trigger image, plus the feeling that the trigger image evokes. The visual part of this is the specific thing that the client sees in the context that causes them to lose control and go into the negative state. In the conversational context, the client's unconscious mind will provide this information. As you ask the client about what they are seeing and hearing, you will see (or hear, in phone coaching) the point at which there is a shift in their state: their posture might change; their breathing might shift; they may sigh; or the tone of their voice may change as, perhaps, tension creeps in. The picture they were seeing in their mind immediately before that change will be the trigger picture that you need.

Of course, it might not always be that simple. For example, you might say: "So you're sitting in the boardroom, waiting for the chairman to arrive, and what happens next?" And the client sighs. So you don't know what happens next, you simply know that something happens that causes them to shift their state and sigh. The easiest way of dealing with this is simply to ask them: "What was that?" They may reply: "What was what?" and you will say: "That sigh." And they will tell you exactly what happens in the mind-movie that makes them sigh. Alternatively, you can ask them to "go over that again for me…" to backtrack the entire sequence.

Again, these questions appear very natural in a conversational setting. People are generally quite happy to talk about themselves and their experiences when the listener is showing an interest in them, in the presence of rapport. Even when you ask them to repeat the story, they will not mind because someone — you — is listening!

3) Break state. In a conversation this is very easy to do. You simply begin to talk about something else, something that is either neutral, or mildly positive. When you do this, you will be checking to make sure that they go back into a state that looks or sounds neutral or slightly positive.

4) Find the outcome picture. After breaking state, you can elicit the outcome picture by asking questions such as: "How will you be as a person when this is so far behind you that it is no longer an issue?" and "How would you prefer to be, as a person, different from how you've been?" and "If you could be any way you wanted, how would that be?" All these questions, while being conversational, ask about the desired identity of the client. You can use whichever version feels most natural to use in your coaching conversations, or you can make up some other version. You could even use a question such as: "How would you like to feel about this?"

Although this question is about feelings, it can still create effective change. You are not asking for a new identity-level picture, so the client may not get the generative benefits of the Swish, but she will still get a change in state which you, as coach, can attach to the trigger and that could well lead to a behavioral change.

While asking about the outcome picture, if you are face to face with the client (not phone coaching), you may wish to hold up your left hand with your palm towards the client. This creates a little "movie screen" on which the client can create the outcome picture. The reason you will generally hold up your left hand, rather than your right, is that it will pull the client's eyes into their "visual create" space. Most people find it easier to create pictures if they look up and to their right (and they find it easier to find pictures from their memory if they look up and to their left).

After you have asked a question to obtain the client's outcome picture, you should sit quietly and wait for a response. The client may need to think for a few seconds in order to find the answer. It's important to realize that the client might provide the answer with their body, not necessarily in words. In fact, the client may not be able to find the words to describe how they want to be. The answer that you are looking for, or listening for, is a shift in the client's physiology into a more positive state. You may see the client straighten up or hear their voice become more confident. You may even hear the client sigh as tension is released.

When you see or hear the client moving to a more positive state, you should both reinforce and validate that change, and also allow the client's conscious mind to catch up with what is going on. What does this mean? Well, to reinforce and validate, you may want to match the physiology and tonality that the client has adopted. You may wish to give an appreciative laugh and say, "That's right!" These reactions will convey that the response the unconscious mind gave was correct. To give the client's conscious mind time to catch up, the coach might ask, perhaps with a chuckle: "What just happened?" The client's conscious mind will likely respond with some insight. They may precede their comments with something like: "Oh, I just realized...." This is exactly where you want to be. When you are doing the Classical Swish, it's important to get the outcome picture in as much detail as possible. But in the Conversational Swish, this might not be possible or appropriate. So it does not matter if the client doesn't describe the picture in detail to you. As long as you know that the client is seeing the outcome picture, that's sufficient.

5) Anchoring the Response. Because you are leading the client through the process in a more covert way, you will need to use covert anchoring. Anchoring is the process whereby a feeling, emotion, or state is linked to, and triggered by, something else in the environment. So for example, if you and your spouse have "your song," that particular music will act as an anchor for the emotional significance and depth of your relationship. The national anthem and the national flag are strong auditory and visual anchors for a state of patriotism. The smell of a certain type of baking may be a strong anchor that takes you back to how you felt when you visited your grandma and she was cooking.

The coach needs to understand how anchoring works and be able to use it effectively in order to do the Conversational Swish. A complete discussion of anchoring is outside the scope of this book. However, we will comment that the words, the tonality, the physiology, and the gestures that the client uses when the client is in their outcome state are the anchors that the coach will use to bring that state back. For example, suppose that, after eliciting the trigger and then breaking state, you asked the Client: "How would you rather be in this situation?" The client looks up and to his right, then sighs and laughs. The coach asks: "What was that?" The client shakes his head and chuckles and says, "I'd be free," while opening his hands, palms upwards. In this case the phrase "you're free," spoken in the client's tonality, together with a gesture of opening the hands, palms upwards, could be an anchor that you could use to re-elicit the outcome state.

Taking the client's words, tonality, and gestures, and using them as anchors, is called "stealing anchors" in NLP. When you have got the anchor for the state, you should test it by doing a break state, then firing off the anchor. To revisit the hypothetical example above, you may break state then ask, using the client's tonality: "And what's it like for you when you're free?" At the same time, you open your hands, palms upwards. You will stress the words "you're free." If the anchor is good then the client should go back into a positive state. This will be reflected in their physiology: their breathing, voice tone, and so on. This lets you know that the anchor is working. If it's not, then you should take the client back into a positive state and look and listen for more anchors to use.

6) Doing the Conversational Swish. You can now run the Conversational Swish by firing off the anchor, waiting for the client to go into a positive state, and then reminding the client of the trigger picture.

Notice that we are suggesting you do the steps of the Swish in a slightly different order this time. In the Classical Swish, you would ask the client to see the trigger picture and then swish in the outcome picture. This time we are firing off the anchor first, and only then reminding the client to look at the trigger picture. You're no doubt asking yourself why we have reversed the order of the steps: The simple answer is that, because you are doing the Swish conversationally, it is more difficult to stop the client from associating with the feelings linked to the trigger picture. If you were doing the Classical Swish, then the client would be focusing instead on the coach's moving hands as she demonstrates the Swish. But in the conversational model, as soon as you remind the client about the trigger picture, they're likely to re-experience the feelings that go along with it. In order to avoid this, put them into a positive state before they see the trigger picture.

A little later, when the Swish has been installed in the unconscious mind, you will reverse the order once more. But for now, you will fire off the positive anchor—"you're free"—and then you will remind them of the picture. So you might say something like: "What will it be like when you're free to view the situation in an entirely different way?"

Begin to back off the anchor as your run through the process a few times.. "Backing off the anchor" is a term that we use in NLP to mean that we begin to use less and less of the anchor each time we fire it. Think of a comedian who tells a joke: as he tells the joke the first time, he makes a certain facial expression and a certain gesture, and perhaps he says a certain key word in the punch line with a particular tonality. The facial expression, the gesture, the key word, and the tonality become anchors for laughter. The comedian later may make a reference to the joke, without telling the whole joke but with the facial expression, gesture, and the key word. Later on, he may simply make the facial expression, gesture, and say the key word and everyone will laugh. He may then simply make the facial expression and the gesture and everyone laughs. Then he just makes the facial expression and everyone laughs. It's the same process here.

The objective of backing off the anchor is to transfer the desired state onto the trigger picture. The trigger picture itself becomes the anchor for the positive state. When you have backed all the way off the anchor and the client is still going into the positive state, then they are doing the Swish on themselves. They are seeing the trigger picture but instead of triggering a problem state, it now triggers a positive state.

7) Test and Future Pace. You should now test and future pace your work. Do another break state, and then simply ask the client to think about a situation in the future when he will see the same trigger picture. If the Swish has been successfully installed, then you will see the client go into a positive, resourceful state. You can then ask the client about how he will behave in the situation in the future, allowing him to practice, or "future pace," the new behavior.

The Conversational Swish is a lot more elegant than the Classical Swish, but it does require a little more practice as a result. You might wish to go to your local NLP practice group (if you have one) and go through the pattern a few times before you try it with clients. To make your practice easier, we have outlined the complete, simplified Conversational Swish below, along with some basic phrases that you can use for each step.

1) Find the context. "What do you want to work through?"

2) Find the trigger image. "Tell me about the last time and place you experienced this. Where are you? What are you seeing, what you hearing, what are you feeling?

3) Test the trigger. "So it's [Tuesday], you're [in the office], and you see [your boss walk in and see his face]…"

4) Break state.

5) Find the outcome picture. [Coach raises her left hand palm towards the client] "So that's how you been, how do you want to be different?" [Invites client to feel resource and create new self-image]. "And when you're [confident], who are you then as a person?"

6) Fire the anchor and then the trigger. "And as you're feeling [confident] and you're [free], and you see [your boss's face] how is it different now?"

7) Back off the anchor while conditioning the Swish.

8) Test and future pace. "So the next time you are in the office and you [see your boss's face]…"

The Conversational Swish allows you to use the powerful Swish Pattern confidently in contexts where it would be difficult to use the standard coaching version. The Swish presented here is versatile and ideal for business settings. Because the Swish is such a powerful pattern, we encourage you to practice being as conversationally creative as possible, so that you have another tool in your repertoire as a coach.

The Social Swish Pattern

In this chapter, we will discuss how to use the Swish Pattern to help friends overcome their problems. The Social Swish Pattern can be used in a similar way to the Conversational Swish. The difference is that in the Social Swish, the friend does not necessarily know that they are being coached. Rather, the coaching will seem like a normal conversation between two friends. The Social Swish can be used whenever a friend is discussing a problem that they have.

Of course, you will have to judge when it is appropriate for you to use the Social Swish to help friends, and when it is not. It will depend, largely, upon the nature of the relationship that you have with the friend in question.

The Social Swish uses the following steps:

1) Re-associate the friend into the problem state, so they begin to re-experience the problem situation. Given that most people love to talk about their problems, this is generally a very easy step, and it's usually the fact that your friend is talking about her problem that brings up the possibility of the Social Swish in the first place. Use the ebb and flow of conversation to associate them into the problem by switching to the present progressive tense ("-ing"), and asking about their feelings. So you might say something like, "Wait, so you are in the office and your boss frowns at you, and how are you feeling when he does that?" As your friend tells her story, notice the words and gestures associated with the problem situation. These

"hot" words and gestures (those that seem to carry the emotional energy of the problem) will be used as anchors to re-trigger the problem situation when doing the Social Swish.

Next, introduce a break state by telling a story that is related to the problem situation but sufficiently different from it that your friend doesn't think you are talking about her. If she does think you are talking about her, then her conscious mind may interfere and she consciously think: "This story is nothing like my situation." One good way to ensure that the story is sufficiently different is to change the gender of the protagonist. So if your friend is a woman, tell a story about a man, while if your friend is a man, tell a story about a woman. A lot of people find it difficult to consciously consider that a story is about them if it is stated to be about somebody of the opposite gender. The story will also introduce the outcome and the outcome picture. If you know that she has an interest in something at which she excels, then you can ask her about this both as a break state, and also to introduce a resource state.

When you've reached the part of the story about the outcome state, you can use a pronoun shift (to "you") to help your friend to envision the outcome picture. Let us suppose that you are telling the story about a friend of yours who had been arguing with his brother, and getting very angry about the situation, but who then finally realized that his brother was acting like a child. In fact, the brother was acting the same way he did when he was in fifth grade. You could then shift the pronoun and say something like, "When you realize that that other person is doing the best they can, given that their social skills are those of a fifth grader, you can begin to realize that you're bigger than that—you're bigger than him—and you no longer need to let him control how you feel. It's time for you to take control of your feelings, and feel at peace even when someone else is acting like a fifth grader." Switching pronouns is something that we do naturally in conversation, but in a coaching environment it allows us to offer direct positive suggestions to our client (or, in this case, a friend).

When you notice your friend's state shift as they envision the outcome picture, you will then use the words, tonality, and gestures of the story to anchor this state. So, in the above example, you may decide to use "you're bigger than that," and "feel at peace," each said with a certain tonality and gesture, as the anchors. You should choose whichever words or phrases you see your friend respond to.

You will perform the Social Swish using gestures associated with the problem, followed by the anchors that you have set for the resource. You will make the gesture associated with the problem and then immediately remove it and make the gesture associated with the resource. Because you're making two gestures in this way, it will be helpful if the gesture associated with the problem is made with one hand and the gesture associated with the resource is made with the other hand. We suggest that you generally make the problem gesture with your right hand, and the resource gesture with your left hand. This will allow you to place the resource into your friend's right visual field – their creative field – and also into their future space, if they are normally organized as regards their timeline. (A full discussion of timelines in NLP is outside the scope of this book, but most people keep their future on their right, or in front of them, and their past on their left, or behind them.)

When you have conditioned the Swish, you can change the topic of conversation. This will act as a break state, and you can return to the problem that your friend shared later on in the evening to test that she feels differently about it now. You will then future pace the new response. This will be the end of the pattern.

Here's a working example:

You meet your friend John for a drink after work. John has clearly had a tough day, and possibly a tough week. You ask him if he is okay and he says: "My boss called me into his office to give me a dressing down about the project I did for him. It was so unfair, as I had no experience in that area and he knew it!" Rather than take the conversation with his boss as feedback, John has clearly taken it as a personal attack and he is seriously pissed. You wonder what will happen the next time John meets with his boss for some more feedback! Perhaps you should offer John a resource—which may make the next conversation between John and his boss easier.

The first step is to re-associate John back into the problem state. Although he has told you about the problem, he has done so from a dissociated position so you do not know whether the anger is what John experienced at the time of the interaction with his boss, or whether it's simply what he feels now, as he looks back on it. In order to re-associate John into the situation, you'd use tools such as shifting into the present tense and spatial awareness of the physical location where the situation took place (so you can gesture toward objects as they were). "Really! So he calls you into his office. Does he at least ask you to sit down?... So you're sitting down, what is he saying to you?..." And so on.

As you speak to John, you begin to set spatial anchors by gesturing to the place where his boss was sitting. In order to do this most effectively, the ideal place to sit is facing towards your friend but slightly to his right. (For most people, the right-hand side represents the future and it also represents their resourceful, creative side. By sitting there, you will find it much easier to lead them into a resourceful state.) So assuming that you are sitting slightly to John's right, you will use your right hand to anchor the position of John's boss in front of him.

At the same time, as John speaks, you will take note of the "hot" words that he uses, and of the tonality and gestures associated with those words. Remember, a hot word is simply a word that John places special emphasis on. Hot words are generally relatively easy to notice once you begin listening for them. In this case, John may use his boss's name with a particular emphasis or tonality, or he may call his boss a jerk (or similar) with a particular emphasis and tonality. These words and their associated tonality are anchors to re-trigger the experience.

Once you have identified the point in the story when John drops into a negative state, and you know the word (or words) that John uses at this point, and the tonality associated with those words, you should test your assumptions by repeating back the hot words to see whether they take John back into that negative state. You only need to test this once! If you test it a number of times you will make John feel much worse.

As you say, "he's a jerk," with the associated tonality, you gesture toward the position of his boss with your right hand.

When you feel like you have sufficient information about the situation in which John found himself, you perform a break state by beginning to tell a true story about you or someone you know—a story that contains a situation that parallels John's situation, but is sufficiently different that it does not appear to be exactly the same story. The secondary purpose of the story is to introduce a more resourceful state. For example, I might tell the story of when I used to fight in martial arts competitions:

"When I was younger I competed in a number of martial arts competitions. These were full contact competitions, no pulling punches. You learn more about yourself fighting with a stranger than you do in six months of training with your friends. In these competitions, you can kick your opponent anywhere above the belt. Kicks below the belt were illegal, of course, but they happened, either by accident or if you happened to be fighting an opponent who didn't respect the rules. So we used to wear a groin protector, a "box." A traditional box is designed to protect the groin from being struck from the front, and on most occasions this was perfectly adequate to protect from accidental blows. However, in one competition, I was fighting an opponent I had never seen. You learn quickly [gesturing with your left hand to anchor the resource of "learning quickly"] who the dirty fighters are, and this guy, he's a jerk [gesturing to your right, the anchor for his boss]. But when you're fighting a jerk like him, actually, these are the fighters who can teach you the lessons you need to learn [gesturing left]. This guy [gesturing right] simply kicked straight into my groin from the ground. My box was not designed to protect from blows that came straight up and this jerk knew it. A second after the impact, I found myself falling to the floor, totally incapacitated. At the time, I was thoroughly pissed with the jerk for the "low blow." However, in retrospect, you realize that there's a lesson to be learned here [gesturing left] from dealing with that jerk [gesturing right]. The lesson is to get good protection, to protect yourself from low blows when you're fighting a jerk, as well as blows that come from the front. Sometimes things happen and you simply have to learn that lesson [gesturing left] so they don't happen again. Jerks [gesturing right] can be your best teachers [gesturing left]!"

Alternatively, you could both break state and introduce a resource state by asking John to tell you about something that he does well: "How was your salsa dancing this weekend? It's amazing that someone can learn to dance as well as you do. You have great footwork—it's amazing!"

Either way, you want to begin to anchor the resource states that you lead John to. As you tell the story, or observe him speaking about his skills, you'll wait to see him change into a good state. You will see him begin to light up as he enters the state. When you see this, you will then set an anchor by using a particular key word with a particular tonality, and making a particular gesture with your left hand at the same time. For example, in the story about the martial arts, the active phrase might be "You can learn the lesson," said with a particular tonality.

Alternatively, as John is telling you his story about salsa dancing, you will wait to see him change state and light up. You will choose as the anchor whatever word or phrase he is saying at this time. Perhaps when he lights up he says something like: "You've really got to know how to move," putting particular emphasis on the word "move." So the anchor might be the word "move," said with the same tonality, or possibly the whole phrase. It won't make a difference whether you choose the single word or the phrase. You have flexibility in how you approach this so choose the one that appears to have the greatest effect on John.

The gesture associated with the positive anchor should be a movement of your left hand, palm out, toward John. It is as if the picture of the martial artist, or the picture of John the Salsa Dancer, is painted on the palm of your left hand and you're moving that picture toward him.

You are now in a position to do the Swish. After all this setup, you essentially have the negative picture on the palm of your right hand, together with a hot word and the associated tonality. This anchors the negative state. You also have a resource state on the palm of your left hand, together with a hot word or anchor phrase for that state.

All you have to do now is to fire off the anchor for the negative state. And then, as you remove that, you will introduce the anchor for the resource state. So, in the above example, you have John's boss on the palm of your right hand, together with the anchor phrase, "He's a jerk," and you have John salsa dancing, together with the anchor phrase "You've really got to know how to move," on the palm of your left hand.

You will then perform the Swish by giving John the suggestion: "When he's a jerk you've really got to know how to move," delivered as follows:

Show John the palm of your right hand as you say, "When he's a jerk…" Then turn your right hand over, so the palm is facing away from John, and begin to move it backward, towards your right, and away from him. Raise your left hand, palm toward John, and begin to move it toward him as you say: "…you've really got to know how to move." As you do this take a look at John's face. If the Swish has been effective then you should initially see a look of mild confusion, which gives way to a positive reaction at the end. Assuming this is the case, simply repeat the Swish to condition it as the night goes on. Each time he mentions his boss you say "That jerk…" [gesturing with your right hand] "…you've really got to learn how to move…" [gesturing with your left hand].

Try the casual Swish out with your family and friends. It's fun to help other people and watch them change for the better, and you deserve a little fun!

The Physical Swish Pattern

Over the last few decades, educators have become aware that students have different learning styles. Some people prefer to learn visually: by seeing pictures, charts, graphs and diagrams, or by watching a demonstration. Other people prefer to learn through sound: by hearing someone speak about a subject and listening to the words, rhythm, and intonation of the speaker. Still other people like to learn kinesthetically: by actually trying something out and feeling their body take on the shape and rhythm of the learning. In this chapter, we will discuss a kinesthetic version of the Swish, which is great for work with kinesthetic learners.

Having the flexibility to use different representational systems (visual, auditory, or kinesthetic) is a wonderful skill for you to develop as a coach. The Hypnotic Swish (see Chapter Twelve) uses sound to trigger the pattern. In fact, when I learned the Swish, many years ago, it was taught using both visual and auditory anchors. I was told to say "swish!" when I wanted the client to change the trigger picture into the outcome picture. Since then, the word "swish" has gathered a wide range of cultural associations relating to gender rights, food, and dancing. As a result, we no longer teach our students to say it when performing the Swish. Instead, we allow the client to create his or her own sound, or use a simple finger snap.

The Kinesthetic Swish uses exactly the same principles as the Classical Swish that we discussed in Chapter Four, but the process has been translated entirely into kinesthetic terms. In the Classical Swish you see the trigger picture moving off into the distance and see the outcome picture approaching, or you see the outcome picture expanding out of the corner of the trigger picture. Sense for a moment the possibility of allowing one feeling to drift away, and replaced by another, or of sensing one feeling expanding out of the corner of another. If this is a little difficult to wrap your mind around, bear with us as we hold your hand through the process.

Here's what you need to know before we lead you through the two variations of the Kinesthetic Swish:

Feelings have a slower tempo than visual scenes. A feeling will last for perhaps ninety seconds, even if you do not begin to intensify the feeling by making pictures in your mind or talking about the situation inside your head. Ninety seconds is simply the time it takes for the biochemical wash that has been triggered by the feeling to move through your mind-body. Because of this, you have to give your client enough time to move from one feeling to another when doing the Kinesthetic Swish.

In terms of NLP eye-accessing cues, feelings are found down and to the right for most people. If you want to get in touch with a certain emotion, then you can allow your eyes to move down and to the right. You can even reach down with your right hand to touch the feelings you want to access. We will be using this accessing when doing the Kinesthetic Swish (although you should feel free to modify if your client is organized differently). Most of your clients will be normally organized. You can calibrate for this by watching their eye accessing during the intake. Are they accessing memories on their left or their right? If the memories are on their right there is a possibility they are reversed organized.

We will offer two different ways of carrying out the Kinesthetic Swish, each using different submodalities. One will be a little slower and gentler, and the second will be faster and more energetic. We suggest that when the outcome state is lower in energy than the problem state, use the slower Kinesthetic Swish (for example, if your client is anxious and wishes to feel calm). For higher-energy outcome states, such as excitement replacing boredom, you might want to use the faster and more energetic Kinesthetic Swish.

Because you are doing the Swish entirely kinesthetically, you do not need to know what the client is seeing as the trigger. In this version of the pattern, it is all about the feeling. However, as with all NLP work, it is better to create change within a certain context, so we suggest that you find both the specific situation within which the client wants to change and the point of synesthesia.

Variation One: The Slow Kinesthetic Swish

Supposing you are with a client who gets anxious, annoyed, agitated, or feels some other high-energy feeling. In conversation, before you formally start running the pattern, you explore with her how she would like to feel and she talks about wanting to be calm and peaceful, relaxed and mellow. In other words, she'd like to feel a lower-energy state than the one she experiences as the problem. Essentially, she wants to slow down and dissipate the energy of her problem state. Higher-energy states tend to overwhelm lower-energy states. Using a slower version of the Kinesthetic Swish will allow time for the higher-energy state to dissipate and the lower-energy state to emerge.

The steps of the slow Kinesthetic Swish are as follows:

1) Associate the client into the context where she wants the change. Uncover the point of synesthesia within this context—what happens that causes her to feel the way she does not want to feel? As usual, you will use present tense language to achieve this. As she discusses the context from an associated position, you will pay attention to her BMIRs, listen for her hot words, and get a grasp on her gestural anchors.

2) Break state. As this is a Kinesthetic Swish, you might want to break state spatially, by asking the client to stand up or move to another part of the room.

3) Ask the client how she would like to feel in the situation. Associate her into this new feeling. So, for example, if she says, "I would like to feel calm," you ask her: "You want to feel calm, and what's it like when you feel calm?" You can build on her response to enlarge the feeling of calm and, as this happens, the words, tonality, gestures, and other BMIRs that she uses will provide the anchors for the state.

4) Ask her to go back into the situation where she wishes to feel this sense of calm. Ask her to see what she sees, and hear what she hears. Allow her to begin to feel the negative state. As you see the BMIRs for the negative state, ask her to reach down with her right hand and unhook the feeling—the anxiety, or whatever the negative state is—and allow it to float away in the sky like a balloon, as, simultaneously, the new state of calm develops. The pacing of the change is pegged to the feeling of calm: The balloon of anxiety will float away at the same pace as the calm grows. Use the anchors for the new state to help her build her sense of calm.

5) Break state. You can take her to the place in the room that represents the break state if you are using spatial anchors.

6) Now ask her to step back into the situation where she wishes to feel the sense of calm. Ask her to see what she sees and hear what she hears. Allow her to begin to feel the negative state and then, again, ask her to unhook the state and allow it to float off into the air only as quickly as the new state, the state of calm, can arise. Repeat the steps as many times as necessary to condition the change. You will know that the change has been conditioned when she is no longer able to access the negative state and instead, she goes automatically into the positive state.

Variation Two: The Fast Kinesthetic Swish

The fast Kinesthetic Swish is an ideal pattern when somebody wishes to have a more energetic state. For example, if your client wishes to be motivated to work out, then they will need energy to do so. The fast Kinesthetic Swish is an ideal pattern to provide this energy.

The steps of the fast Kinesthetic Swish are as follows:

1) Associate the client into the situation that she wants to change. Let's say that she feels lethargic. What does she see, or hear, or feel in this context that lets her know it is time for her to have more energy? Use the present tense and pay attention to her BMIRs as she enters the low-energy state.

2) Break state. As with the slow Kinesthetic Swish, you may use a spatial anchor to break state by asking her to move to another place in the room.

3) Ask your client how she wants to feel differently in the situation. Perhaps she wants to feel excitement. Associate her into this state of excitement. If her neurology and physiology are not accustomed to high-energy states, then pacing and leading will be extremely important. This means that you, as the coach, have to get into the high-energy state first in order to lead her there. Once she associates into the high-energy state, pay attention to her

BMIRs as, once again, these will provide anchors for the state.

4) Ask her to step back into the situation where she needs this high-energy excitement. As she begins to slip back into the low-energy lethargy, suggest that she reach down to the right, with her right hand, and grasp the new state of excitement. As she now has a hold on this state, she can pull it up and through her body by moving her right hand strongly and steadily up toward her left shoulder. It should look and feel as if she is throwing a cloak over her left shoulder. Use anchors to help her associate into the excitement. The movement should be faster and more energetic than in the slow Kinesthetic Swish but should still give her enough time for her energy to change.

5) Break state by asking her to move to the point of the room occupied by the break-state anchor.

6) Now ask her to step back into the situation where she needs that excitement. Once more, calibrate if she begins to slip into the state of lethargy, and get her to reach down with her right hand and pull the state of excitement up toward her left shoulder. The movement should be slow and steady. Use the anchors for excitement to assist the process. Break state and repeat as many times as necessary until she automatically goes into a state of excitement whenever she begins to feel the lethargy.

The Self-Coaching Swish Pattern for Personal Success

The Swish Pattern is ideally suited for use as a self-coaching technique. If you haven't already, read Chapter Four, which outlines all the steps of the Classical Swish and the necessity of each one. Once you have all that information, you are ready to practice becoming the new you.

Unlike many NLP patterns, the Swish is very easy to run on yourself because it is based around the manipulation of pictures within your mind. As long as you can visualize the outcome picture, you can easily run the Self-Coaching Swish. Because the first part of the Swish involves seeing what you actually see in the outside world when you are in the situation in which you want to feel differently, all you have to do is go into that context and look around you. Look at what it is that would normally make you feel less than resourceful and then simply imagine the outcome picture swishing up in front of you. It is as simple as that! Now we will go through each step in detail.

Overview of the Self-Coaching Swish Pattern

The Swish as a self-coaching tool follows the same basic steps as the Classical Swish. First, you select a context or situation where you want to change how you feel or behave. The Swish can actually be practiced in this physical location, as long as you can go there and have a minute or two for the required mental rehearsal. If you can't do this—for example, if a specific person at work has been making you feel unresourceful and you can't go into their office and rehearse the Swish—then go to a similar environment and imagine they are there, or simply find a quiet place to imagine. What you do not want to do is to try and practice the Swish in a real-time environment. For example, if you want to stay calm when your boss is yelling, don't wait until he is actually yelling in your face to practice! Practice first in a low-pressure environment that you control, so that your unconscious mind will be trained to do the heavy lifting later, in the real situation.

Now you are ready to find the trigger picture: what you see through your own eyes when you are in the problem context or situation and immediately before you begin to feel unresourceful. The easiest way to find the trigger picture is to go to the environment and slowly look around. As your eyes rest on the trigger picture, your unresourceful feelings will begin to increase. There could be a number of different trigger pictures to deal with in any one environment, and if so, simply do the Swish Pattern on each trigger separately.

Now you will take a moment to create the outcome picture. If it is easier or more convenient, you can create the outcome picture before you go into the environment. The outcome picture is simply a picture of you as you would want to be in the situation: your ideal self. This outcome picture should be amazing and inspiring. Make the picture big and bright and totally compelling. The one thing you must make sure of is that the picture is attractive to you. It should make you think: "Yes! I want to be like that!" The outcome pictures should include you with any added abilities you would like to experience in the context, and also everything else that you will have when you are able to perform the outcome behavior effortlessly.

Whatever you feel is attractive and compelling to you should be part of the picture that you use.

Now you can do the Swish by exchanging the two pictures. If you are doing the Swish in a place other than the environment where you want the change, then practice by visualizing the trigger picture. Now notice some well-defined spot within the trigger picture where you can place the postage stamp-sized outcome picture. For example, if you are doing the Swish in the context of a business interaction, you could choose the forehead of the person you are talking to. In your imagination, shrink the outcome picture to the size of a postage stamp and place it on the spot you have chosen. Now perform the Swish as usual. Have the outcome picture spring out from that spot, growing as it does so into a life-sized and three-dimensional picture of you in full Technicolor. If you wish, you can step into this image and see how fantastic it feels to know that you are already becoming this new you!

If you are doing the Swish in real time, in the place and situation where you'd like to change, then you will not have to imagine the trigger picture — it will actually be there in front you. In this case, simply look at the trigger and imagine that the stamp-sized outcome picture has been placed at some specific point in the scene in front of you. Now once again, do the Swish as usual by imagining the outcome picture springing out and becoming life-sized, three-dimensional and Technicolor. Once more, if it is appropriate, step into the image and feel how good it feels to know that you are already becoming this person.

Repeat the Swish a number of times until you feel yourself completely entering into that state of total resourcefulness.

Summary of the Self-Coaching Swish:

1) Select a context.

2) See the trigger picture, either in real life (by going to the actual physical location) or in your imagination. This is what you see immediately before you want to be your best.

3) Create a picture of the ideal you, the outcome picture.

4) Embed the outcome picture somewhere in the trigger picture.

5) Imagine the outcome picture exploding out of the trigger picture and becoming life-sized in front of you.

6) If appropriate, step into the outcome picture.

An Example of the Self-Coaching Swish

Peter is a salesman for an office machine company. He wishes to feel totally confident each time he makes a sales presentation.

When asked, "What do you see immediately before the sales presentation begins?", after a little thought he identifies being in a situation where he is sitting across the desk from his prospective client, and his client is frowning and saying, "We already have all the copiers we need." Although Peter believes that he can bring a superior solution to any prospective client, he reports feeling a drop in energy when he hears this (which is frequently). Now Peter has both the context and the trigger picture for the Swish.

Peter's outcome picture is of the Peter who is confident; knowledgeable about his field, his company's products and their advantages to his competitors' products; focused on the prospective client's needs; and politely determined to educate the prospective client about the pros and cons of his company's products.

However, the outcome picture should also have other attributes based upon the following questions: "Why do I want to get this account? What do I achieve in winning this account? Why do I want to be a success in my company and my field? Who will I be as a person when I am a total success in this field? How will I look then?"

As he asks himself these questions, Peter begins to form a picture of himself as proud of his profession and his role in the company. He sees himself standing taller and speaking with more authority not only to his colleagues, but also to his clients and prospective clients. Because he is more successful, he sees himself as no longer feeling the pressure to make any particular sale. As a result, he can relax into the process of acting as a consultant to his clients and prospects, educating them about the true cost of their office machines—including not just leasing costs, paper, toner, and maintenance, but also the cost of reprinting inferior copies, paper jams, downtime, and other factors. In this picture, he sees himself as more of an educator than a salesman. As a result of his financial success, he sees himself better dressed and driving a better car. He also sees himself looking healthier and fitter because he will have more time to take care of himself and go to the gym. By the time he is done with the process, he is extremely excited about the new Peter he sees in the picture.

Peter passes a small park on his way to work every day, and he decides to initially practice the Swish for five minutes each day while sitting in the park. He sits down in the park, imagines one of the prospective clients he is going to see that day—imagines sitting in their office, across the desk from them. Peter then takes a postage stamp-sized copy of his outcome picture and places it firmly on their forehead. Then he imagines hearing them tell him that they have all the office machines they need, and at that point in time the new self-image springs out of their forehead and appears—life-sized, three-dimensional and Technicolor—in front of him. He blanks the screen and repeats this a few more times. He also runs the pattern with some of the prospective clients he has visited in the past, particularly those that gave him the hardest time. When he's done, he walks on to work. After one week of practicing the pattern in the park, he begins to use it in real time when he is actually sitting in front of the prospect. As he is sitting there, he imagines seeing the postage stamp-sized picture of the new Peter, right in the middle of their forehead. He then has the image spring out of their forehead into the space between them. Peter is very happy with the results and is closing more sales.

However, he still has trouble with some of his accounts and still gets the old feelings of doubt. When asked which accounts he has the most difficulty with, Peter says it is with large prospective customers, when there is a lot of pressure to close the sale, and also some of his existing customers who intimidate him. When asked, he reports that the old feelings of doubt arise before he walks into their office. In fact, he begins to have these feelings as soon as he imagines walking into their building. Peter now begins to practice the Swish as before, but this time based on the trigger picture of the front door to their building: Peter sees the front door and imagines his outcome picture embedded in the corner of the front door. The outcome picture then springs out of the door, becoming life-sized, three-dimensional and Technicolor in front of him; he steps into it, taking it with him as he enters the building. He repeats the process as he enters the door to the prospect's office suite, and also on the client's forehead as they first greet him. He continues to run the Swish from their forehead as they sit in the meeting. He uses the same outcome image for each Swish. He also practices each Swish in the park in the morning, as well as in real time as he visits each client. His state of confidence in these high-pressure meetings increases dramatically.

After a few weeks of practicing the Self-Coaching Swish in this way, Peter finds that it begins to take place automatically; he will approach his client's office building ready to do the Swish, and find that he has already done it on a more unconscious level. At this point Peter begins to incorporate the Self-Coaching Swish into other areas of his life, including his golf game!

Troubleshooting the Self-Coaching Swish

In this section, we will discuss what can go wrong in using the Self-Coaching Swish. If you are not benefiting from the wonderful changes that the Swish can bring about, it's likely to be for one of the following reasons.

If you decide to do the Swish in real time — for example, as you are walking into your client's office — then this should not be the first time you do it. Doing the Swish only in real time is like an NFL team practicing only when they run onto the field for the Super Bowl. You should practice the Swish in a low-pressure environment first, before you get to the client's office, so that your unconscious mind and your neurology is primed to do the Swish when the time comes.

Make sure that you use the Swish sufficiently early in the process that leads up to the undesired state. For example, it's no use having a great sense of confidence when you stand up to make a presentation if you have behaved like a gibbering idiot for the previous twenty minutes! Break each situation down into the triggers that could lead to a negative state, and run the Self-Coaching Swish on each one in turn.

For example, a sales presentation might be broken down into how you want to feel and behave in the following situations:

>The pre-sales presentation rehearsal.
>
>Entering the client's building.
>
>Entering the client's office suite.
>
>Being introduced to the client's team.
>
>Making the presentation.
>
>Answering questions at the end.
>
>Saying goodbye to the client.

You can't expect to get the results you want by doing the Self-Coaching Swish only once or twice. Remember the value of repetition for the purposes of rewiring your brain. The more times you do the Swish, the stronger you are making the associated neural pathways. If you only do the Swish once, then you can expect only limited results.

If you are doing the Swish in real time, you must remember to actually do it when you need it. If you don't do it, it won't work! And if the situation in which you need it is one where you usually feel nervous, then you may very well forget to do the Swish. Make it a regular habit to check in on your own state. Ask yourself: "How am I feeling right now?" This is probably the single most important thing that you can do to transform your life. The simple process of stopping, checking in with your feelings and, if they are not what you'd like them to be, making a decision to feel another way, is powerful. This practice of choosing how you want to feel will create spectacular changes in your life. It demonstrates to you that you have choices about how you feel and gives specific instructions to your unconscious mind to feel and behave in a certain way. You'll find that giving specific instructions to your unconscious mind is exactly what it wants—remember, though, to give those instructions stated in the positive—"I want to feel confident"—not in the negative: "I don't want to feel nervous".

Remember also that, for most people, the Swish is a visual pattern, so make the pictures, don't just tell yourself how to feel. It is difficult to change your state by simply telling your unconscious mind in words how you want it to be. There are a couple of reasons for this: first of all, the unconscious mind is not as comfortable with words as it is with pictures. Words are primarily used by the logical, left brain, and the executive, conscious mind. The second reason is that, when using words, we can easily slip into the negative impact of saying: "I don't want to feel...." For example, "I don't want to feel nervous." Stating your desired outcome in this negative way makes things very difficult for your unconscious mind to understand. Your neurology will be unable to respond. Here's an illustration of the problem: If we were to say to you, "Don't think of a pink elephant," you'll find that the only way you can avoid thinking of the elephant is to first actually think about it, and then attempt to stop thinking about it. Similarly, the only way your unconscious mind can process the idea of "don't feel nervous" is by first feeling nervous, and then trying to stop feeing that way. It's much more effective to show your unconscious mind how you want to feel by giving it a positive outcome picture that it can move toward without conflict.

The key to running the Swish on yourself is to make sure that it is operating on an unconscious level. If you are simply doing it as a logical, cognitive exercise, the process will not be sufficient to create a deep unconscious change in your feelings and behavior. How do you know if it's operating at an unconscious level? You should feel a physiological shift when you do the Swish and the outcome picture expands or leaps out in front of you. Your will body let you know it is being reset into a new state. For some, this feels like an opening up in the chest, but for you it may be different.

Making the Self-Coaching Swish Part of Your Everyday Routine

Each and every time you walk into a room, you are walking into a new situation and you may need to change your state. The state you want to be in when you see your boss may be very different from the state you want to be in when you speak to your client, which will be different again from the state you want to be in when you see your family. Each time you walk through a doorway you have the opportunity to do a Swish and step into a new state.

This Swish is such a fantastic pattern for controlling and maintaining your own state that you may wish to consider the following exercise:

Make each and every doorway that you walk through the trigger picture for a new Swish.

Create some awesome outcome pictures—new self-images. Make one for the office, another for your client's office, another for your home, another for the golf club, another for the gym—however many you want.

Choose an outcome picture and embed it into each doorway you walk through. So if you are entering your office, you would have the outcome picture for the "ideal-you-in-the-office" waiting in the doorway for you to walk through. As you approach the door, have the outcome picture expand into the doorway, waiting for you to walk through and take it with you.

When you walk through the doorway, you walk through the outcome picture. It wraps around you like a new skin as you absorb those new qualities and feelings.

If you do this exercise on a regular basis, then your unconscious mind will internalize the process on its own and will then begin to do the process by itself each and every time you walk through a doorway. Each doorway will automatically trigger the state that you need in that situation. Of course, in order to do this, your unconscious mind needs to have a sufficient amount of experience in choosing the appropriate states. You have to consciously do some work in setting this pattern up so that your unconscious mind knows what is required of it. But once you have done that, you will have created an awesome generator of positive states for yourself!

When making the outcome picture big, consider making it slightly larger than life-size so that you can easily step inside it if you wish to.

The more you practice the Self-Coaching Swish, the more it will become incredibly generative for you. Before you know it, your brain will automatically be shifting less resourceful pictures into wonderfully powerful outcome pictures. In this way, the Swish is one of those exercises that has the potential to not only change your reactions in certain contexts but to change your whole life!

The Swish Pattern for Business

Because the Swish Pattern is visual, it's quite easy to run on yourself in real-time. We have included several examples of how you might use the Swish as a self-coaching pattern in a business context in the previous chapter.

The Swish is also a great pattern to use in a business context with colleagues or clients. People in a business context usually have specific goals, as well as specific stresses and frustrations. These stresses and frustrations provide ample trigger pictures, and their goals provide great outcome pictures. Furthermore, you will find that your colleagues and clients will be quite generous in giving you the information that you need to run the Swish. Below, we will describe two situations in which you could use the Swish in your business.

Before we go on, though, remember that the Swish Pattern should be used to improve the lives of those around you. It should not be used for unethical purposes such as persuading somebody to buy a product they do not want or need. Using NLP in this way is manipulative and may jeopardize your business relationships.

Using the Swish Pattern to Coach Your Team

Businesses are fond of setting individual goals. Large organizations and companies often spend a lot of time and effort setting goals for each individual employee. Unfortunately, these goals are often written down, or entered into the system, and not looked at again or considered until it's time for a performance review. Thus the primary reason business goals are not achieved is that they are disconnected from day-to-day activities and the company employees are not emotionally involved in the goal-setting.

The Swish Pattern offers a unique method for taking the goal-setting process, involving employees on an emotional level, and attaching their goals to their everyday environment. The context in which they work—their day-to-day environment—becomes the trigger picture. Who they will become as result of achieving their goals becomes the outcome picture. Attaching the outcome picture to the trigger picture using a Swish Pattern will remind your employees of their goals on a day-to-day and hour-to-hour basis, and on a deeper emotional level. As a result, their goals are much more likely to be achieved.

Here is the procedure for using the Swish Pattern to set corporate goals:

1) Set the goals in the usual way.

2) Make sure that each employee is emotionally committed to his or her goal. This is done by asking the question, "Who will you be within the organization, and within your career, as a result of achieving these goals?" You should see the employee become more animated, perhaps smiling and speaking faster, when they talk about goals that they are emotionally committed to. If there is not a physiological shift the coach can explore with the employee whether the goal is truly hers or if it is what she thinks her goal should be.

3) Lead the employee to build a visual self-image of how they will be when they have achieved their goal and reached the next level within the organization and their career. This can be done overtly or covertly, depending upon the relationship with the employee, the personalities of those involved, and the culture of the company or organization. For example, if you wish to help the employee build this new self-image, you might ask, "When you have achieved these goals, who will you be within the organization and within your career? What will you be doing that is different from what you are doing now? If I were to come and see you one year from now, and you have achieved your goals, what will I see?" You'd give the employee time to answer, and then repeat back what they have just told you, saying something like: "That sounds great. So I would be seeing...." As you describe this new self-image back to the employee, you should see the same animated emotional response as before.

You can anchor this new self-image using the employee's words and tonality, as well as raising your left hand with your palm turned towards the employee. (Anchoring in this way is discussed more fully in Chapter Thirteen.) Test the anchor by breaking state and then raising your left hand again while you describe how the employee will be when she has achieved her goal. You will know the anchor is effective if you see her go back into the positive state. If not, go back to finding out what she truly wants and the hot words and gestures associated with that.

You can now do the Swish by reminding her of what she will see at the time that she needs to take action to achieve her goal, and then immediately reminding her of her outcome. For example, if her outcome is to be promoted to supervisor with the ability to "make a difference," and one of her goals is to complete the monthly billing on a timely basis, you might say, "Each time you see those monthly billing reports, you'll know that [raising your left hand] you're making a difference, and completing those reports is a step toward your goal of being a supervisor." In this case the Swish is contained within the unconscious instruction to link the monthly billing reports with 'making a difference'.

If you are a manager or other business leader, using the Swish in this way will make a huge difference to the performance of your team.

Using the Swish with Business Customers

The Swish can also be used with customers to help achieve a sale. Again, we cannot stress enough that NLP techniques such as the Swish should only be used in an ethical way. If you try to use these techniques to manipulate your customers, you risk generating a lot of buyer's remorse, which loses future business! That said, one way of using the Swish with customers is to construct a trigger image representing whatever problem they are facing, and an outcome image of you and your product having solved their issue.

Let's take the example of Mark, a consultant in the healthcare industry. Mark provides technology solutions that assists healthcare providers with their billing procedures, and ensures that they are in compliance with governmental regulations. Failure to bill on a timely basis means his clients do not get paid, while making a mistake with the billing could lead to a government investigation. Mark is visiting a prospective client. First, Mark begins to clarify the trigger picture. He might say something like: "Many of my clients have concerns about their billing procedures [setting the context]. They look at the reports generated by their billing system [identifying the trigger picture] and [sighs to check if the trigger picture generates a negative state] they're not sure if they're capturing all the value they should be, or, worse, if they're inadvertently overbilling. So you may find your business has cash flow issues, or you could be in serious trouble with the government. This is all a big headache for people like you, who would prefer to spend their time helping patients." Depending upon the response of his client, Mark will have identified the trigger picture. If the client does not respond then Mark will move on to some other portion of the billing cycle.

Mark may now spend some time asking the prospective client how her business could be improved, and what that would look like to her. This will provide Mark with some ideas about the outcome image, as well as various anchors for the outcome state (the client's hot words, including the tonality and gestures).

Next, Mark will break the negative state by describing what his company does. He may give some impressive facts and figures about the effectiveness of his solution. Mark will now generate the outcome picture. He will do this by talking about the healthcare organizations he has helped. He might say something like: "My clients experience a faster billing cycle and greater cash flow, which saves them much of the time they used to spend billing. Let me tell you about one of my clients who has a practice similar to yours and is using our solution..." Mark will then go on to describe this client, building up a picture similar to what Mark will expect to see if the prospect engages him to provide his solution. While describing the outcome picture, Mark will make sure that his solution is part of it. Mark will anchor the positive state his client goes into while listening to the story, using certain key words and gestures.

It is quite possible that Mark will close the sale there and then. If not, Mark will attach the outcome image to the trigger image using the Swish Pattern. He will say something like: "I realize you are very busy, and that you are focused on providing the best care to your patients; when you're looking at the reports generated by your current system, consider whether our solution is right for you—to help you focus on providing care while generating healthy cash flow...." [Mark continues to fire off the anchors for the positive state.]

The Swish is a fantastic way to improve your business. Using it within your company allows you to help motivate your employees in a way that leads them to achieving the specific goals set for them. The Swish also helps you to better serve your clients and customers by allowing you to communicate to the client just how you will fulfill their particular needs in a way that is highly ethical. When employees and clients are realizing their goals on a regular basis, the value of your company increases immensely.

The Swish Pattern for Dealing with Difficult People

We will all occasionally find ourselves having to deal with difficult people. As practitioners of NLP, we seek to be at "cause," which means accepting responsibility for how we feel. We take steps to choose how we feel—to choose our state—and then to enter that state. Fortunately, as practitioners of NLP, we have a lot of tools to allow us to control our own state, and one of the most powerful of these tools is the Swish. In this chapter, we will describe how to use the Swish effectively when dealing with difficult people, either for our own benefit or for that of our clients. As a coach, you can use the Swish to make yourself feel good when dealing with your own difficult clients (if you have any). I'm sure you will agree that this is a great tool to have!

Difficult people tend to make us feel less than resourceful—otherwise they wouldn't be difficult! We may feel annoyed when we are with them, or frustrated, or angry, or upset. If, instead of feeling annoyed, we felt calm, then things would be much easier for us and probably for them as well. If, rather than frustrated, we felt happy, then they may lighten up too. If, instead of feeling angry, we felt peaceful, then our experiences will be much more pleasant, and this pleasantness would be shared with them. Rather than running a destructive cycle—whereby we feel frustrated working with that person, which feeds into how they react to us and then into how we react to them—we can begin to run a virtuous cycle, whereby we feel more relaxed and comfortable working with them, which then feeds into how they react to us and how we react to them. When we master the Swish, we can always feel completely resourceful in the presence of difficult people; we can feel calm, confident, or however else we want to feel.

The Swish for Dealing With Difficult People

Adapting the Swish Pattern for dealing with difficult people is easy, as it follows the Classical Swish Pattern very closely. Here are the steps:

> 1) Select the person who makes you feel less than resourceful. For the purposes of this exercise we will call this person the DP (Difficult Person).

> 2) Think of a context—a time and place—when you were with the DP. Where are you? What is happening? What are you seeing? What are you hearing? Notice how you're feeling. Run this experience as a movie where you are seeing out of your own eyes. Pay particular attention to what the DP is doing immediately before you get the feeling. What do you notice? What are you paying attention to immediately before you get that negative feeling? This is the trigger.

> 3) Do you smell popcorn? (In other words, break state!)

> 4) Consider how you want to be in the presence of the DP. Perhaps you can make a movie of yourself feeling good and dealing with this person in a very resourceful way.

Sometimes we make movies like this after the fact, and in the movie we make some snappy comeback that puts the other person down. This is not the best movie to have if you want to improve the interaction you have with the DP. What you want to create is a movie that results in a win-win situation. How can you walk away from this interaction, having made that person feel good and feeling good yourself? To create this win-win movie, ask yourself the following questions: What is important to you about your interaction with this person? Why are you interacting with them at all? Think about what interacting with this person does for you. For example, if this is somebody at work, then ask yourself: Why are you working? If there is no reason for you to interact with this person that is more important than the difficulty they create for you, then perhaps you should stop interacting with them!

Perhaps you are working in order to make money to support and protect your family. When you realize what your larger outcome is, you realize what is really important about your interaction with the DP. Then you can ask yourself the question: "When I'm supporting and protecting my family at my best, who am I then, as a person?" This is the self-identity that we will install using the Swish. So when you are supporting and protecting your family, when you are a father or mother, what is really important to you? What are you believing about yourself and the world? What capabilities do you have when you realize you are acting to support and protect your family?

When you have all of this, construct the new self-image picture of your ideal self. In our example, the image would be of the father or mother supporting and protecting his or her family, with all the values and beliefs and capabilities that that implies, and doing whatever he or she needs to do to get the job done.

Alternatively, you could use the archetype method described earlier in the book. Think of a character that you know from a movie, a book, history, or think of somebody from your own life who would have the skills necessary to deal with the DP in a totally resourceful way. Again, aim for a win-win outcome to the interaction. We are not seeking to put anybody else down, or to "win" if it's at someone else's expense.

When you find a person who can deal with this sort of situation easily, an ideal archetype, make a picture of them in your mind. You can even find a picture on the Internet if it helps. Take a look at the picture. What is it about the archetype that grabs your attention? What is it about their posture? What is it about their facial expression? What do those things reveal about them? What do those things reveal about their capabilities, the ones that would help in dealing with the difficult person? What is it that is important to them? What do they believe about themselves and the world? What other capabilities do they have? What emotional strength do they have? As you look at the picture, begin to notice everything about that picture which reflects their beliefs, their values, and their capabilities. When you have done this, begin to transform the picture into a picture of your ideal self, the ideal you. Take on their identity in the situation involving the difficult person. Adopt their beliefs and values in this situation. Notice that you also have their capabilities and their emotional strength. Make that picture big and bright; make it three-dimensional; make it into a movie, with sound. Make it panoramic, so that it wraps around you. When you see the picture of your new self, you should feel fantastic.

Doing the Difficult-People Swish Pattern

We are now ready to do the Swish using the two pictures we have constructed. The trigger picture is the DP doing whatever it is that they do immediately before you begin to feel bad. The outcome picture is the new you, either the you who is embodying your own highest ideals—those that are really important to you and that cause you to interact with the DP—or the archetype. Either way, this is the person you are already becoming! Shrink the outcome picture down to postage-stamp size. Take a look at the trigger picture. It will contain the face of the difficult person. Take a look at the spot right in the middle of their forehead. Now embed the outcome picture there.

Now we're ready for the Swish: imagine you are in the context when you last interacted with the difficult person. Imagine being back there, seeing what you are seeing and hearing what you are hearing. Notice the difficult person, and notice that small postage stamp-sized spot right in the middle of their forehead. Now swish that small picture until the image of your new self appears in bright Technicolor, in three dimensions, right in the space in between you and the DP. See that image of your new self and notice how good you feel. If you want, you can step forward into that image. Notice how good it feels to be that new person.

Now blank the screen. One more time, go back to that context when you last interacted with the difficult person. Imagine being back there, seeing what you're seeing and hearing what you're hearing. See the person with the image right in the middle of their forehead, and swish that image so that the new you appears between you and the difficult person. Blank the screen and repeat. One more time, blank the screen and repeat.

This time, blank the screen and repeat, and then allow the movie to play out. Notice how your interaction with the person is different this time. Notice how you can continue to feel resourceful in their presence. Notice how these resourceful feelings allow you to behave in a different way. Notice how your behavior impacts the difficult person, and how they begin to be less difficult. Notice how they behave in a different way.

Now take a different context, a different time and place when you interacted with this person. Again go back to that time, seeing what you're seeing and hearing what you're hearing. Notice the difficult person, and notice that they have the image embedded in their forehead, the image of the new you. Swish that image until the new you appears in between you and the difficult person. If you wish, you can step into the new you and feel how good that feels. Blank the screen and repeat. Once more, blank the screen and repeat. And finally, one last time, blank screen and repeat, but this time allow the movie to play out, noticing how it's different for the new you, with these new resources.

Pick another context and repeat the process. In fact, repeat the process with as many contexts as you can think of. At some stage, your unconscious mind is going to generalize the process so that each time you think of this person, you feel resourceful. This is when you know that the Swish is fully installed in your unconscious mind.

The Future Pace

Now think of a time in the future when you may have to interact with this person. Step into that experience and notice what you're seeing and hearing. Now imagine that person appearing in the scene. Notice that they have that little image right in the middle of their forehead. It's almost like somebody has slapped a postage stamp on there! Notice what happens. Don't be surprised if you suddenly find yourself feeling totally resourceful. You may find that each and every time you interact with this person in the future, your interactions are very different from what took place in the past. You might find that your experience changes so completely that it begins to change the difficult person. From now on, your interactions with that person will be a lot more positive, and a lot more fun.

The Swish Pattern for Smoking and Other Habits

As we have already mentioned, the Swish is an excellent pattern to use with clients who smoke, bite their nails, eat unhealthy food, or engage in other unwanted behaviors and habits. Indeed, in the early books about NLP written by Richard Bandler, the Swish was normally described in the context of either smoking or nail-biting. Because of this, we will spend some time discussing the Swish in the context of changing habits.

There are many reasons that the Swish is an excellent pattern for changing bad habits:

>1) It is very quick and easy to do. This means that the Swish can be incorporated into a larger piece of change work within a coaching session. The Swish only takes five or ten minutes to do, and within that time the Swish can be performed numerous times to condition the change.

>2) The Swish is very easy to construct in the context of a habit. The trigger picture is easy to find. It will be precisely what the client sees before engaging in the unwanted behavior. The outcome picture will be a picture of the client having found the control to overcome the habit.

>3) The conditioning power of the Swish makes it extremely effective in the context of a habit.

Desire for a Cigarette and Desire for Change

There is another reason that the Swish is such a powerful pattern for changing bad habits such as smoking. Richard Bandler has stated that the desire for cigarettes can be mapped onto the client's desire to become a better person in the outcome picture. When the smoker is thinking of the trigger picture—often the packet of cigarettes—he enters into a state of desire, a state that can be focused onto any outcome. It could be smoking a cigarette, or it could be becoming a new person. In this way, it is the client's desire to smoke that propels him toward his own future self. Using the Swish in this way allows the problem—the desire for the cigarette (or to bite a nail, or whatever it may be)—to become a resource.

Finding the Trigger Picture

When dealing with bad habits and compulsions, the trigger picture will be what it usually is: whatever the client sees through their own eyes immediately before they engage in the behavior.

For a smoker, this may be the cigarette as it approaches his mouth, or the pack of cigarettes being offered to him, or perhaps the newsstand where he buys his pack of cigarettes.

For a nail-biter, this will likely be a picture of his hand as it approaches his mouth.

For someone who eats too many doughnuts, for example, it will be the doughnut approaching his mouth, or possibly the box of doughnuts, or possibly the doughnut store sign, which he sees before he goes to buy his doughnut.

The trigger picture can be big and bright and appealing to the client. This will help to generate the state of desire, which can be mapped onto the desire to become a new person as discussed above. When the client looks at the trigger picture, he should feel the desire to engage in the unwanted behavior (in contrast to the Swish for difficult people, in which the trigger picture will not be appealing, and may be darker, although it will likely also be big).

Finding the Outcome Picture

The outcome picture will reflect the client's ability to overcome the bad habit. Therefore, at a minimum, when the client sees himself in the outcome picture, he will see a person who has self-control. So the outcome picture is likely to be a picture of himself with self-control and also with the physical benefits of the change. For example:

For the smoker, the outcome picture may be a picture of the client with better skin, better teeth, and clearer eyes. He will be breathing more easily, moving more, being generally healthier, and he will have self-control.

For the nail-biter, the outcome picture may be a picture of the client with attractive nails, more self-confidence, and more self-control.

For the doughnut-eater, the outcome picture may be a picture of the client looking slimmer and healthier, being more physically active, with better skin and more self-control.

Running the Swish for Bad Habits

The Swish itself will be run like a Classical Swish, as described in Chapter Four. The client will see the trigger picture, embed the outcome picture in one corner or in some detail of the trigger picture, and then be guided by the coach to do the Swish using the slingshot technique or simply by shrinking the trigger picture whilst expanding the outcome picture. It is the moving away or shrinking of the trigger picture that will push the smoker away from the act of smoking. It is the moving toward, or the increase in size of the outcome picture that will pull the ex-smoker toward her future self.

For habits and compulsions, the Swish should be done quickly to maintain the state of desire. In fact, the faster the Swish is done, the more likely it is that the client will feel the desire that she used to feel for the cigarettes or the nail-biting, now transferred onto a future self.

Combining the Swish with the Six-Step Reframe

When a client has a bad habit or compulsion, there is almost always a secondary gain. A secondary gain is something that the smoker gets out of the act of smoking. It could be relief from stress or boredom; it could be something to do with being social or "cool;" or it could be something completely different. This secondary gain may be so important to the smoker's unconscious mind that it causes her to hold onto the smoking habit—unless she finds another way to satisfy the need that is currently being addressed by the secondary gain.

Usually, in order to satisfy this need, the smoker will find another behavior instead of smoking. This is called "symptom substitution." If the substitute habit is much less harmful than the original one, then the switch may not be an issue. For example, the ex-smoker may go out and buy a squeeze ball to relieve her stress. But the new behavior may be worse than the original habit, in which case the coach or hypnotist has not done the smoker any favors by helping her. For example, the ex-smoker may unconsciously begin to eat when she would otherwise have smoked. If the eating gets out of control, then she may gain considerable weight, which would also have serious adverse consequences for her health. By addressing one bad habit, she has simply created another.

The classic NLP pattern for dealing with secondary gain is the Six-Step Reframe. We are not going to describe the steps of the Six-Step Reframe it detail, however it utilizes symptom substitution by allowing the client to select a new behavior to substitute for the old one. The new behavior is then subject to an ecology check — meaning that the coach will prompt the client to check that the new behavior will be good for all aspects of the client's personal and professional life. This will prevent inappropriate substitutions. The new substitute behavior can then be combined with the Swish by incorporating it into the outcome picture so that, by the end of the process, the client will see herself with the benefits of having stopped the compulsion and also engaging in the new behavior.

The Swish can be applied to any bad habit or compulsion. The steps outlined above can be translated to deal with any problem behavior, as long as the outcome picture of how they want to be different includes the concept of self-control. Here's an example of using the Swish for smoking and nail-biting.

An Example of a Swish with a Six-Step Reframe for Habits

The trigger picture for the Swish Pattern in the case of a smoker will usually be the pack of cigarettes, or occasionally the sight of a cigarette approaching the smoker's mouth. The usual considerations apply with respect to picking an appropriate trigger image. For example, if the trigger image is the sight of a cigarette approaching the smoker's mouth, this presupposes that the smoker has already bought a pack of cigarettes, has taken the cigarette out of the pack and has maybe even already lit the cigarette. So using the cigarette approaching the mouth as the trigger image attaches the outcome image to a point in the smoking process that is quite advanced. A better choice might be to use the pack of cigarettes as the trigger picture. This approach presupposes that the cigarette has not yet been taken out of the pack, and it therefore inserts the outcome picture earlier on in the smoking process.

Of course, using the pack as the trigger presupposes that the client has already gone out and purchased a pack of cigarettes. Therefore, you may wish to use the newsstand where the client typically buys their cigarettes as the trigger picture. This attaches the Swish and the outcome picture at the earliest stage of the smoking process: the point at which the client actually buys the cigarettes. Of course, the client may not buy cigarettes at all; she may be given a cigarette by a friend. So you may have to do the Swish Pattern on a number of triggers: the cigarette, the pack of cigarettes, the cigarette kiosk where she buys her cigarettes, as well as her friend who offers her cigarettes. You may also wish to do the Swish Pattern on events in the client's life that would previously have caused her to smoke. For example, if she smokes because of stress, then you may wish to do a Swish Pattern to deal with the causes of stress (see below).

The outcome picture for the Swish Pattern will be the image of the client as she will be, a healthy non-smoker. This new and improved healthy non-smoker will likely breathe more easily, have clear eyes and clearer skin, smell better, and look generally healthier. She may also be taking more exercise and therefore may look fitter as well as healthier. In addition, the new and improved healthy non-smoker will have more self-control, more personal power, and will be overall a more self-actualized person. This may show up in various ways in the picture depending upon how the client views her new self. For example, the new and improved healthy non-smoker may stand in a more self-confident way, hold her head in a more self-confident way, or speak in a more self-confident voice. We have already talked about her breathing being easier and deeper.

You may also wish to deal with ecology issues in the outcome picture. For example, if you have also done a Six-Step Reframe with the ex-smoking client, then you will have helped her to identify alternative behaviors to satisfy the positive intention of the smoking. If smoking was used to relieve stress, then you'll help her identify alternative behaviors that will help with relieving the stress and/or maintaining a state of calm and relaxation. When building the outcome image, you can include these alternative behaviors. If the Swish is being done on, for example, sources of stress that caused the ex-smoker to smoke, then the new self-image will be relaxed. This may show itself in a more relaxed posture, more relaxed behavior, and a generally more relaxed attitude. The same outcome image can be used for each of the Swishes, if multiple Swishes are used for multiple contexts. Once the trigger picture and the outcome picture have been created, then the Swish can be performed in one of the usual ways.

Nail-biting is another issue that responds very well to the Swish because it is usually automatic. The client generally notices that they are in the process of biting their nails, or that they have bitten their nails—but they don't notice when the process starts. This indicates that nail-biting tends to be unconscious, and therefore installing an unconscious process such as the Swish works very well.

The trigger picture for a nail-biter will typically be the sight of the hand and fingers and fingernails approaching the mouth. This will almost always be what the nail-biter sees when he has dropped into his unconscious nail-biting program. The nails of a nail-biter are usually bitten down to the quick, and they are not usually considered to be attractive. When working on this pattern, you can contrast the unattractive nails of the nail-biter with the attractive nails of the reformed nail-biter, as seen in the outcome picture. In addition, the new and improved ex-nail-biter in the outcome picture will have self-control, and self-actualization. After all, if the client is able to make this change in his life, just imagine what else he could do. The client should be encouraged to see himself as actualized, and to visualize those characteristics in the outcome picture.

As in the case of smoking, if you have done a Six-Step Reframe on the nail-biter, then he will have identified the positive intention of his habit and also one or more positive alternative behaviors that he will carry out instead. You will encourage the nail-biter to include these behaviors in the outcome picture so that it unconsciously reminds the client about them.

When you have identified the trigger picture and the outcome picture, you can perform the Swish in any of the ways previously discussed. The different methods of performing the Swish will have slightly different effects in the case of a nail-biter. If you use the Slingshot Swish, then you will tend to pull the client's attention away from their nails as the slingshot moves into the distance. In contrast, the version of the pattern that uses image size as the submodality will tend to make the outcome picture appear between the client and their fingernails. Bear in mind that one Swish method may be more effective than another for your client, depending on their preference.

Stepping into the Future

Now you've had a chance to learn about the Swish—and, hopefully, as you have been reading this book—you've been able to practice the Swish on yourself, your clients, colleagues, friends, and perhaps even on total strangers. Each of these interactions represents a moment in time when you can hold the space long enough for the other person to become more than they thought they could be. They are able to step into their potential. Each of these interactions is an opportunity for you to transform the life of another person. Many more such opportunities lie in front of you.

At the end of any NLP pattern we do a final step called the future pace. During the future pace we would invite the client to imagine stepping into the future with their newfound skills and abilities, feeling confident in the changes and able to practice new self-beliefs. So as you step into the future, we invite you to travel to a time and place where, previously, you might not have had the resources, but now things are different. Now you are different. And as you step into that time and place, you also step into the new you. So we might say something like:

"Imagine taking the knowledge and the skills you have learned and stepping forward into the future, to a time when they will be of benefit to you and others. And I don't know if this time will be later today, or tomorrow, or in the days and weeks ahead, but think of one specific occasion now. Take the time you need to think of that time and place. When you have it in your mind, and as you imagine being there with these newfound skills and abilities, seeing what you see, and hearing what you hear, you will begin to feel those new feelings of confidence.

"And you realize that you do have the knowledge and the skills to make a difference in this situation. You can transform the lives of those around you, and you can transform your own life. And the amazing thing about transformation is that you never know how far a change may go. It may seem small at first, but it can sweeten into a new path of infinite possibility.

"As you find yourself in this time and place, with these new skills, this new knowledge and this new confidence, you begin to realize that you know what to do and you know how to do it. You begin to behave in new ways, ways that change everything, ways that affect everyone around you in exciting and positive ways."

And then we might invite the client to think of another time, saying something like:

"And you can begin to imagine, now, another time when these new skills and abilities, this new confidence, will be useful to you and those around you. And because this is the second time that you will use these new skills and abilities you will be feeling even more confident, and you will be even more effective. You will see even more clearly what needs to be done, and how to do it.

"And as your conscious mind continues to consider more times and places where you could use your new skills, you may find something interesting taking place within your unconscious. Your conscious mind deals in logical, step-by-step processes, but your unconscious mind can deal with many things at once. So as your conscious mind continues to process in one way, your unconscious mind can process in a different way, a way that is much faster, considering each and every time in the future when you can use these new skills and abilities and considering what things will be different."

When you start to create future memories in this way, memories of what can be, you begin to program your unconscious mind for success. So please remember to future pace. It will make all the difference.

ABOUT THE AUTHORS

Shawn Carson is founder and co-director of the International Center for Positive Change and Hypnosis. He is an NLP/HNLP and hypnosis trainer and he runs a thriving training center in New York City. Shawn is a consulting hypnotist and works with private clients for trance-formational change. Originally from the UK, Shawn now lives in Manhattan, New York.

Jess Marion is a trainer with the International Center for Positive Change and Hypnosis and founder and director of Philadelphia Hypnosis. She is a NLP/HNLP and hypnosis trainer, NLP/HNLP Master Practitioner, and consulting hypnotist. Jess runs a busy private practice in Philadelphia and lives and works in New York and Philadelphia.

ACKNOWLEDGMENTS

First and foremost, we are indebted to the co-founders of NLP, Richard Bandler and John Grinder, without whom nobody would be practicing in this wonderful discipline. We would most like to thank the genius of Richard Bandler who, we understand, is the developer of the Swish Pattern.

We would like to thank John Overdurf who, directly or indirectly, taught us everything we truly understand about NLP. John stands as a shining example of a self-examined life. We stand in awe of John's compassion and skill, and truly believe that he is "doing it right."

We'd like to thank our hypnosis teachers, Melissa Tiers of the Center for Integrative Hypnosis in New York City, and Igor Ledichowski from streethypnosis.com. In our model of the world, NLP and hypnosis are two sides of the same coin; you cannot properly practice one without the other. Melissa and Igor taught us what trance is.

We would like to thank our wonderful editor, Nancy Rawlinson, for her hard work and patience.

Finally, we would like to thank our business partner, Shawn's lovely wife Sarah, for her invaluable support and suggestions.

Glossary

Anchor: An external stimulus such as a touch that you feel, a gesture or image that you see, or word or sound that you hear, which leads you to feel a certain emotional state.

Archetype: A person or character who embodies an idealized behavior or state.

Associated: Being inside a mental picture, looking out of your own eyes, seeing what you see, hearing what you hear, and feeling what you feel in the situation.

Coach: Someone leading another person through a process of change, for example by using the Swish Pattern.

Conditioning: The process of repeating a pattern a number of times until it becomes embedded in the neurology of the brain and the physiology of the body.

Dissociated: Seeing yourself in a picture as if looking at a photograph of **yourself.**

Eye Accessing Cues: Eye movements that provide a guide to, and that influence, what is happening inside the client's mind.

Future Pace: Inviting the client to imagine multiple future instances in which they are acting and feeling resourceful when experiencing the trigger for the old issue.

HNLP: Humanistic Neuro-Linguistic Psychology, a set of skills, techniques, and patterns based upon NLP and developed by John Overdurf and Julie Silverthorne.

Leading: When the coach makes small changes in the client's physiology and speech to help move them away from an unresourceful state and into a resourceful one.

Mind Reading: Believing one knows what someone else is thinking, believing, and feeling.

Modeling: Adopting the physiology, state, values, and beliefs regarding behavior, as well as the strategy, of someone who does something excellently.

New Behavior Generator: A technique in NLP whereby a new behavior is installed in a client by getting them to step into the image of a role model who is already able to perform the behavior.

NLP: Neuro-Linguistic Programming, a set of skills, techniques, and patterns developed by Richard Bandler and John Grinder in the 1970s.

Normally Organized: The most common way people use their neurology to organize their eye accessing cues and their sense of time. A normally organized person will access memories by looking to the left and imagination by glancing to the right. In terms of time, the past will be either to the person's left, or behind them. The future will be to their right, or in front of them.

Outcome Picture: In the context of the Swish, a dissociated picture of the client as the client wishes to be.

Pacing: Matching the client's physiology, tonality, and language to create a strong sense of rapport.

Rapport: The foundation of successful communication. It shows empathy, respect and acknowledgement of the other person's style of communicating, both consciously and unconsciously. It is used to help clients change, as well as to build stronger relationships. Rapport may involve adopting the client's words, posture, and gestures.

Resources: Any positive, helpful feelings or states such as confidence, calmness, excitement, peace, and love.

Secondary Gain: The hidden benefit obtained by the client from their negative habit or behavior.

Six-Step Reframe: An NLP exercise that elicits the positive intent behind seemingly problematic behavior, and during which the client's unconscious mind is invited to generate other, positive ways for that intention to be met.

Slingshot: A particular method of performing the Swish Pattern in which the trigger picture is sent out into the distance and the outcome picture returns as if on a piece of elastic.

Submodalities: The qualities of our internal representations, be they visual, auditory, or kinesthetic. Submodalities can include size, brightness, distance, location, volume, movement, intensity, and the number of dimensions.

Swish: An NLP pattern involving chaining together two pictures. The first picture is a trigger for the problem, and the second picture is what the client wants, or the outcome.

Testing: The process used to determine if a piece of coaching was successful.

Trigger Picture: In the context of the Swish, an associated picture of what the client sees immediately before he or she has the problem.